"[Lahiri's] observations are as plentiful as they are enlightening."
—JULIANA UKIOMOGBE, *Elle*

"[*Translating Myself and Others*] is about the consequences of the apparently simple act of choosing one's own words. . . . [The] book also contains a hope for the liberating power of language."
—BENJAMIN MOSER, *New York Times*

"Passionate [and] thoughtful."
—FRANK WYNNE, *The Spectator*

"A wry collection."
—ADAM RATHE, *Town & Country*

"[Lahiri's] voice is a strong one in the current campaign to give translators more recognition. Her candidness about the hardships of translation and her enthusiasm for its rewards make you want to hear more from these fascinating figures, who spend so much time in others' voices but have not lost the use of their own."
—CAMILLA BELL-DAVIES, *Financial Times*

"Anyone interested in the art of translation will be engrossed by *Translating Myself and Others*."
—MARTIN CHILTON, *The Independent*

"Lahiri's ruminations on translation are relatable and luminous."
—CARMEN ACEVEDO BUTCHER, *Christian Century*

"Fascinating and insightful."
—LAUREN ELKIN, *American Scholar*

"This cool, detached book bristles with life and love."
—JOHN SELF, *The Observer*

"These deeply thoughtful meditations . . . illuminate the art of literary alchemy."
—*Saga*

"Eloquent. . . . [Lahiri] explores what it means to be a translator, how translating enhances her identity as a writer and vice versa, and how these multiple identities are mutually enriching."
—HAYLEY ARMSTRONG, *In Touch*

"[A] portrait of intelligent, sensitive and deeply humane curiosity. . . . Inspiring."
—JAMES KIDD, *South China Morning Post*

"Readers . . . will find themselves immersed in a voyage of discovery not just of what makes Lahiri the writer and the translator tick, but of how these two facets or 'containers' inform, extend, challenge and ultimately re-create her."
—LILIT ŽEKULIN THWAITES, *Sydney Morning Herald*

"Lahiri achieves the task of portraying her profound love for linguistics and the ways languages give new life to one another in translation."
—AMANDA JANKS, *Zyzzyva*

"Jhumpa Lahiri is a marvel, a writer with the courage to renounce virtuosity for the sake of vulnerability, experiment, and growth, and it's been wonderful to watch her love affair with the Italian language unfold. In these essays, she delves deep into the fertile interstices of and between languages, giving us a book rich with insights and pleasures."
—SUSAN BERNOFSKY, author of *Clairvoyant of the Small: The Life of Robert Walser*

"A remarkable account of Jhumpa Lahiri's journey from English to Italian and back. Her pages on the myth of Echo are the most poignant and eloquent account of the translator's art that I have ever read."
—MICHAEL F. MOORE, translator of Alessandro Manzoni's *The Betrothed*

"With this collection of elegant essays, Jhumpa Lahiri makes her career as a writer of two languages and, increasingly, as a translator between them seem less an eccentric adventure than a necessary one. No man is an island—and no language, either."
—DAVID BELLOS, author of *Is That a Fish in Your Ear? Translation and the Meaning of Everything*

"In these stunning essays, Jhumpa Lahiri brilliantly investigates the fluctuating borders between writer and translator, language and identity, artist and art. Her intellectual and deeply personal inquiries—reminiscent of Hannah Arendt, Virginia Woolf, and Susan Sontag—challenge us to engage with our own mysterious and metamorphic relationship to language and who we are."
—JENNY McPHEE, translator of Natalia Ginzburg's *Family Lexicon*

TRANSLATING
MYSELF AND
OTHERS

Translating Myself and Others

Jhumpa Lahiri

PRINCETON UNIVERSITY PRESS

Princeton and Oxford

Requests for permission to reproduce material from this work
should be sent to permissions@press.princeton.edu

Published by Princeton University Press
41 William Street, Princeton, New Jersey 08540
99 Banbury Road, Oxford OX2 6JX

press.princeton.edu

First paperback printing, 2023
Paper ISBN 9780691238616

The Library of Congress cataloged the prior U.S. edition
of this book as follows:

Names: Lahiri, Jhumpa, author.
Title: Translating myself and others / Jhumpa Lahiri.
Description: Princeton : Princeton University Press, [2022]
| Includes bibliographical references and index.
Identifiers: LCCN 2021047885 (print) | LCCN 2021047886 (ebook) |
ISBN 9780691231167 (hardback ; acid-free paper) | ISBN 9780691238609
(ebook) Subjects: LCSH: Lahiri, Jhumpa. | Translating and interpreting.
| Self-translation. | Translators—United States—21st century—Biography.
| BISAC: LANGUAGE ARTS & DISCIPLINES / Translating & Interpreting
| BIOGRAPHY & AUTOBIOGRAPHY / Women | LCGFT: Essays.
Classification: LCC P306.92.L34 A3 2022 (print) | LCC P306.92.L34
(ebook) | DDC 418/.02092—dc23/eng/20211206
LC record available at https://lccn.loc.gov/2021047885
LC ebook record available at https://lccn.loc.gov/2021047886

British Library Cataloging-in-Publication Data is available

Editorial: Anne Savarese and James Collier
Production Editorial: Ellen Foos and Jaden Young
Text Design: Amanda Weiss
Production: Erin Suydam
Publicity: Jodi Price and Carmen Jimenez
Copyeditor: Anne Cherry

This book has been composed in Signifier (Klim Type Foundry).

in multas igitur voces vox una repente
diffugit, in privas quoniam se dividit auris,
obsignans formam verbi clarumque sonorem.

—LUCRETIUS, *DE RERUM NATURA* (4.565–7)

Therefore one voice is suddenly dispersed
Into many voices, since it divides itself
Into separate ears, stamping onto them
The form of the word and its distinctive sound.

—RONALD MELVILLE, TRANSLATOR

(CONTENTS)

Introduction

A translation dilemma is among my earliest memories. I was five, seated at a large table with many other children in a kindergarten classroom, making cards for Mother's Day. Together we folded stiff sheets of white paper, and constructed and pasted pink crepe-paper roses with green stems to the cover. The assistant teacher circled the table, spraying some perfume into each of our roses. Inside the card, we all had to handwrite the same message: "Dear Mom, happy Mother's Day." This part of the project stymied me, given that my mother was not "Mom" but "Ma." I was embarrassed to insert the Bengali term I used and knew her by—the one she recognized and responded to. I was also reluctant to resort to the English term, which sounded foreign to me, and would have certainly alienated, even offended her.

The memory is still fresh, though I can no longer remember what I chose to write inside the card. Revisiting that dilemma now, in 2021, it occurs to me that it has just as much to do with the act of writing as it does with translation. In other words, as soon as I learned how to write in English, which was one of the two languages I knew and spoke as a child, I simultaneously intuited the central and complex role that translation was to play. It also reminds me of the role, just as central and complex, that my mother was to play in my life as a writer, both as subject and inspiration.

In 2000, the year after my first book of short stories, *Interpreter of Maladies*, was published, I wrote an essay called "To Heaven without Dying" for the online magazine *Feed*. I was still new to the world of writing, still getting used to the idea of having become a writer in the first place. In that essay—the first occasion I had to assess my evolving creativity entirely on my own terms—I speak of being born into a "linguistic world split in two." I refer to my writing, in English, as a form of cultural translation, and to some of the stories in that collection as a "translation of India." Reflecting on writing short stories in English about characters who talk in Bengali in my head, I note the need to translate their dialogue, thus turning them, falsely but necessarily, into English speakers. I conclude, dramatically, "I translate, therefore I am."

Over twenty years later, this statement has only intensified in significance. I risk quoting myself not only to signal that this is a book about translation, but to acknowledge that I have been thinking about translation for my entire conscious life. As that early essay already makes clear, becoming a writer in English meant becoming a translator as well. And yet, I was a translator before I was a writer, not the other way around. As a graduate student, for my master's thesis, I'd translated some short stories by the great Bengali writer Ashapurna Devi, thanks in great part to my mother's willingness to read them out loud. I would tape-record her, play back the cassettes, and work off our homemade audiobook, given that Bengali is a language I speak and understand but do not read with sophistication or ease. Before that formal project, in college, I had studied Latin and Ancient Greek. Once I'd learned enough grammar to be able to read texts, reading and translating melded into a single experience. That form of reading, dynamic and double, more active than passive, has remained the gold standard for me. But in fact I was translating even before that, even before I knew how to read. I was raised speaking and living, simultaneously, in English and Bengali, and this meant translating between them, constantly, for myself and for others.

The current volume gathers together my written thoughts about translation over the past seven years. I have spent these years teaching creative writing and translation at Princeton University, but before I came to Princeton I was living in Rome, where my linguistic landscape dramatically transformed, and Italian emerged like a new island in an archipelago, just as Ovid describes in the *Metamorphoses*: "and what deep water had covered / now emerges as mountains, dotting the sea with more Cyclades."[1]

In Italy I began writing directly in Italian. I recounted this experience in *In altre parole*, my first book in Italian, later translated into English as *In Other Words*. The first essay in the present volume, "Why Italian?," is a coda to that book and also a point of departure, deepening and shedding further light on the basic question of why, after becoming a writer in English, and writing four works of fiction in English, I chose to write in Italian instead. I did not translate *In Other Words* myself; at the

---

[1] "quosque altum texerat aequor / exsistunt montes et sparsas Cycladas augent" (*Met.* 2.263–64). Translation in progress by Yelena Baraz and Jhumpa Lahiri.

time, I was putting all my energy into writing in Italian, and not translating anyone, never mind myself, into the language I know best.

But this was all to change in 2015. I left Rome and began teaching at Princeton, where I felt immediately and instinctively drawn to the world of translation. It was in and among other languages at Princeton that I felt most at home. "In Praise of Echo," written in 2019 while I was back in Rome on sabbatical, grew out of the first literary translation workshops I taught at Princeton. And just as I was embarking on the teaching of literary translation, I became a bona fide translator myself, taking on the task of turning a novel called *Lacci* by Domenico Starnone, whom I'd met in Rome, into English.

Lacci (which became *Ties*) led to *Scherzetto* (*Trick*) and *Confidenza* (*Trust*); I have included my reflections on the experience of translating each of these novels, all of them by Starnone, in the present volume. I translated all three of them at Princeton. Another project I undertook at the university was the compiling and editing of *The Penguin Book of Italian Short Stories*, an anthology I was inspired to assemble due partly to the fact that numerous Italian short-story writers I'd discovered and wanted to share with my Princeton students, in English, had either not been translated to my satisfaction, or were only available in dated translations, or had not been translated at all. As I worked on that project, I realized that several of the authors in the book were not merely authors but also translators. I was struck by how many Italian writers of the previous century devoted considerable time and energy to practicing and promoting the art of translation, not only for personal mentorship and influence, but for furthering the essential aesthetic and political mission of opening linguistic and cultural borders, and of introducing readers to works they would not be able to access otherwise. As

I contemplated the contributions of these author-translators, I was grateful that my creative life had taken a turn, and that I could now count myself among them.

Alongside the translation of Starnone and other Italian authors, I was gravitating, after arriving at Princeton, toward the supremely disorienting and, some say, controversial act of translating myself. When I first attempted this, very early on after starting to write in Italian, I quickly withdrew my hand, feeling that English, with an unexpected snarl, had snapped at me. But in 2017 I set aside my fear and translated a short story I'd written called "Il confine," titling it "The Boundary."[2] That experience paved the way, eventually, for the translation of *Dove mi trovo*, a novel I wrote in Italian, and which I turned into *Whereabouts* in English. Though I've done it once, I don't know if I will translate another of my Italian books into English. It poses a particular challenge, though not an entirely unpleasant one. In any case, "Where I Find Myself" takes stock of the process of self-translation, at least in one specific instance, and stops to reconsider words like *original, authentic,* and *authorship.*

By now I feel inevitably drawn to a series of authors who lived, read, thought, and worked among different languages. Whether I am reading Aristotle or Gramsci or Calvino, the theme of translation is what rises to the surface and engages me most. Translation, at the moment, has become my primary heuristic key. I have included, here, a set of essays I think of as a casual dinner party comprised of a handful of authors I've been thinking about recently, seated together at a table with translation serving as a centerpiece. At the end of each essay, I specify its origin, as well as the location and the language in which I wrote it. I do so in order to emphasize that this is, essentially, a

[2] *The New Yorker*, January 29, 2018.

bilingual text composed in two distinct geographical settings, Princeton and Rome. I wrote three of the ten essays in Italian, and others were drafted in a hybrid of English and Italian before I converted them fully into English in their final form. The three Italian essays—"Why Italian?," "*Lingua* / Language," and "Calvino Abroad"—have been translated either by myself or by others who did the lion's share before I sat down to adjust this or that.

For those who read and study Italian, I have included, in an appendix to the book, the essay on Calvino in its original form, as well as Domenico Starnone's Italian translation of my English essay "Where I Find Myself."[3] Given that I speak throughout this book about the experience of writing in Italian and about translating myself, or being translated, into English, these versions provide concrete examples of how an English-language writer migrates into Italian and back again. In the English essays, unless otherwise indicated, all translations are my own.

After deliberating on how to order the essays, I have done so chronologically. I hope that this arrangement serves to tell its own story: to recount how my thinking about language and translation has evolved from project to project, and how my creative, personal, and intellectual perspectives have gradually, inevitably altered as a result. Placing the essays in chronological order allows me to chart my progress, and reminds me of how rapidly and radically things can change. "Why Italian?" was written before I had ever translated anything from Italian to English. By the time I wrote "Calvino Abroad," I had translated

---

[3] Starnone also wrote the introduction, in Italian, to the latest American edition of *Interpreter of Maladies*, which I subsequently translated into English, so we have now become both translators and interpreters of one another.

the works of more than half a dozen Italian authors, Calvino among them, and had also translated my own Italian work.

My reflections over the past seven years have grown thanks to a great many authors who have written about the theory and practice of translation before me. They are a new and stimulating element in my reading diet, and now that I have the pleasure of teaching translation, I often assign texts about this intricate and enigmatic subject to my students, discovering and analyzing them together in the classroom. While I do not engage explicitly with other theorists and writers on translation in this book, my suggestions for further reading acknowledge my indebtedness to the texts that have influenced and guided me, and will perhaps enable readers to place this volume in a broader scholarly context.

The afterword that closes the book opens a new door—which is fact an old door—and talks about my current translation project, which is to co-translate Ovid's *Metamorphoses* from Latin into English with Yelena Baraz, my colleague in the Princeton Classics Department. I quoted from the *Metamorphoses* earlier in this introduction, and you will discover that I refer to it in more than one of the essays. In the world of translation, Ovid's great poem, for me, is the sun. No other text I know illuminates what translation does, means, or is with equal power, and without it as an ongoing point of reference, my understanding of life, language, and literature would go dark.

Translation has transformed my relationship to writing. It shows me how to work with new words, how to experiment with new styles and forms, how to take greater risks, how to structure and layer my sentences in different ways. Reading already exposes me to all this, but translating goes under the skin and shocks the system, such that these new solutions emerge in unexpected and revelatory ways. Translation establishes new rhythms and approaches that cross-pollinate the process of contemplating and crafting my own work. The attention to language that translation demands is moving my writing not only in new directions, but into an increasingly linguistically focused dimension. In 2021, I published *Il quaderno di Nerina* in Italian,[4] a work that combines verse and prose. I would never have begun writing poetry without the intimate exposure to the Italian language that only translation can provide; this shift was particularly surprising given that I have never written poetry in English.

I have assembled this book not only because I have become a translator in the past seven years, but to reiterate that I have always been a translator. To be a writer-translator is to value both being and becoming. What one writes in any given language typically remains as is, but translation pushes it to become otherwise. Thanks to translation—the act of one text becoming another—the conversation I have been seeking to have with literature for much of my life now feels more complete, more harmonious, and far richer with possibilities.

Before I engaged seriously with translation, something in my life as a writer was missing. At this point, I can no longer imagine not working on a translation, just as I cannot imagine not working on—or thinking of working on—my own writing. I think of writing and translating as two aspects of the same activity, two faces of the same coin, or maybe two strokes, exercising distinct but complementary strengths, that allow me to swim greater distances, and at greater depths, through the mysterious element of language.

---

[4] I provisionally call this "Nerina's Notebook" in English, as it does not yet have an English incarnation.

(1)

Why Italian?

After moving to Rome in 2015, I sought to respond to this question. For many years, I had studied Italian from afar, without ever having lived in Italy. The desire to speak it every day, to plunge into a new idiom, to encounter new people and a new culture, led me there. Once I arrived, I wanted nothing other than to express myself in Italian as often as possible. But nearly each time I opened my mouth, I would hear the same question: *Why do you speak our language?* I tried to explain. I said that I'd studied Italian because I loved it, that I felt the need to have a relationship with the language. I said that I'd learned to speak some basic Italian thanks to private lessons in New York. Given that I had chosen to do so without any practical need, and without any obvious connections—familial, personal, or professional—my explanation didn't satisfy. People told me, *You're of Indian origin, were born in London, raised in America. You write books in English. What does Italian have to do with any of that?*

The more I explained, the more people I met in Rome persisted, intrigued, a little stupefied: *But why, exactly?*

While no one expected me to speak Italian, I didn't expect the question. It was reasonable enough to ask, but it put me a bit on the defensive. Why was it, I wanted to ask my interrogators, that I needed to justify myself?

In truth, the reason I couldn't respond to their question was because I had never asked it of myself. I didn't think that my growing dedication to the Italian language was anything unusual. Before coming to Italy, I'd never paused to consider what it meant. I was more interested in the how than the why: how to speak the language better, how to make it my own.

It was only in Rome that I started to ask myself: *Why Italian?* I wrote *In altre parole* (*In Other Words*) to give a definitive response, both to others and to myself. It was born from the realization that I am a writer without a true mother tongue; from feeling, in some sense, linguistically orphaned. But that book, which I wrote in Italian, complicated the situation considerably.

After *In Other Words* was published, first in Italian and then in English, the question of *Why Italian?*—which I'd hoped to resolve—only turned more frequent and urgent. I was asked by friends, journalists, writers, readers, editors, Italians, Americans, everyone. The question has led to a realization: that while the desire to *learn* a new language is considered admirable, even virtuous, when it comes to *writing* in a new language, everything changes. Some perceive this desire as a transgression, a betrayal, a deviation. What I did—distancing myself suddenly from English, passing precipitously into Italian—tends to trigger resistance, diffidence, and doubts.

Everyone wants to understand the genesis, the motives, the implications of my choice. Some people ask me, *Why Italian instead of an Indian language, a closer language, more like you?*

The short answer remains: I write in Italian to feel free. But when I would talk about the book in public, during speeches and interviews, I felt repeatedly forced to defend, to justify this liberty. To provide a key, to clarify the issue.

If *In Other Words* needs a key, it's the book itself. I began with a metaphor that led me to another, and then another. That was how my thinking unfolded. In the book, my slow but stubborn learning of Italian is a lake to cross, a wall to climb, an ocean to probe. A forest, a bridge, a child, a lover, a sweater, a building, a triangle. If, by the last page of the book, *Why Italian?* remains incomprehensible, I am to blame.

Once my first attempt to write in Italian was behind me, I undertook another. From time to time new metaphors came to mind, even if I didn't look for them anymore.

In the days immediately preceding the release of the book, while I was preparing to discuss it in public, I discovered three new metaphors that I found particularly fruitful, ambiguous, and evocative. Had it been possible, I would have added three chapters to *In Other Words*. The present essay serves as a sort of "external" epilogue.

For the last metaphors, all three, I was indebted to my readings in Italian. They came to me from two writers, both of whom are central points of reference for me. One has passed away, the other is still living. One was little known outside of Italy and the other is known all over the world, though no one knows her real identity. I discovered the former in Rome, the latter in the United States, before moving to Italy. They are two Italian writers, both women, with two distinctly different styles. The first is Lalla Romano. Elena Ferrante is the second.

I had never heard of Lalla Romano before coming to Italy. I learned about her thanks to an article published in *La Stampa*, written by Paolo Di Paolo. It's not easy to find the works of Lalla Romano in Italian bookstores. But Paolo di Paolo was a liaison between me and Antonio Ria, Romano's second husband, who kindly sent me a large package of books.

I read several titles in one go: *Nei mari estremi* [In extreme seas], *Maria, Inseparabile* [Inseparable], *L'ospite* [The guest], *Le parole tra noi leggere* [Light words between us]. I was struck straightaway by the singular force of her taut, meditative, sorrowful writing. I was drawn to her dry, essential style. I admired her concise sentences, brief chapters, and distilled language.

The evening before I discussed *In Other Words* for the first time, in Venice, I was reading *Le metamorfosi* [The metamorphoses], Romano's first book of prose, published in 1951. It spoke to me; even the title was a word I had used for one of the chapters, and was one of the metaphors of my book. Romano's work, which essentially recounts a series of dreams, represented a definitive turning point for the author, signaling her passage from painting to writing—from one means of creative expression to another. This, too, struck a chord. At the end of the fourth part, the author recounts a dream that she calls "Le porte" [The doors], cited in its entirety here:

The door is not yet closed, but it is about to shut.
One of the panels, tall and massive, falls slowly upon
the other. I run and succeed in passing through.
Beyond it is another door, identical to the first. This
one is also on the point of closing; this time, running,
I also succeed in passing through. There is another
one, then another. One must be very quick in order
to get there on time. Nevertheless, I hope I can always
pass through, seeing as no door is closed. But one
must keep running, and I am getting increasingly
tired: I'm starting to lose my strength. The doors

appear, one after the other, all of them the same. I can
still pass through; but it is useless. There will always
be another door.[1]

I read Romano's dream as an existential nightmare: the tale
of an ominous, frustrating, and difficult road. It indicates a
trial, disorienting and exhausting. It describes a sense of dis-
may, desperation, and finally, defeat. The doors represent an
ongoing effort, a journey without end: the condemnation of
finding oneself forever waiting, on the outside, in a kind of
purgatory.

This paragraph—this dream—made me reflect at length on
the excitement and anguish of my path to Italian. For decades,
ever since I immersed myself in the language, ever since I fell in
love with it, I've struggled to open a series of doors. Each one
leads me to another. The more I confront them, the more I pass
through them, the more others appear, needing to be opened,
to be overcome. This is how the study of a foreign language—
an asymptotic trajectory—proceeds.

In order to conquer any foreign language, one needs to
open two principal doors. The first is comprehension. The
second, the spoken language. In between, there are smaller
doors, equally relevant: syntax, grammar, vocabulary, nuances

[1] "La porta non è ancora chiusa, però sta per chiudersi. Uno dei battenti,
alto e massiccio, ricade lentamente sull'altro. Corro e riesco a passare.
Di là c'è un'altra porta, uguale alla prima. Anche questa è sul punto di
chiudersi; anche questa volta, correndo, riesco a passare. Ce n'è ancora
un'altra, poi un'altra. Occorre molta prontezza per arrivare in tempo.
Tuttavia spero che potrò sempre passare, dal momento che nessuna
porta è chiusa. Ma bisogna continuare a correre, e io sono sempre più
stanca: comincio a perdere le forze. Le porte si presentano, una dopo
l'altra, tutte uguali. Posso ancora passare; ma è inutile. Ci sarà sempre
ancora una porta," p. 149.

of meaning, pronunciation. At this point, one gains relative mastery. In my case, I dared to open a third door: the written language.

Bit by bit, as one studies, the door to comprehension swings open. The spoken language, apart from a foreign accent and some mispronunciations here and there, also opens with relative ease. The written language, certainly the most formidable door, remains ajar. Since I started thinking and writing in Italian only at the age of forty-five, I knocked on this door quite late, and it creaks a little. Although it welcomes me, it keeps odd hours, and is rather unpredictable.

The more I write in Italian, the more I feel in turmoil, suspended between my old knowledge of English and the new door in front of me. I'm forced to acknowledge that there is a distance between me and both languages. Sometimes I fear that the next door will be boarded up. Writing in another language reactivates the grief of being between two worlds, of being on the outside. Of feeling alone and excluded.

In *In Other Words*, I refer to a door as well: it's the door of our first home in Rome that, one evening, our second evening in Rome, refused to open. It was an absurd moment, a nightmare with a significance perhaps too obvious, but which took time to fully understand.

Each door has a dual nature, a contradictory role. It functions as a barrier on the one hand; as a point of entry on the other. The doors keep urging me forward. Each leads me to a new discovery, a new challenge, a new possibility. How wonderful that, in Italian, the etymology of the word for door, *porta*, comes from the verb to bring, *portare*, which also means to raise, *sollevare*, "because Romulus, in mapping out the walls of the city with a plow, raised them in the very place where the gates [*porte*] would be constructed."[2] Although a door remains something inanimate and concrete, the word's root conveys a decisive and dynamic act.

Confronting a foreign language as an adult is a considerable challenge. And yet, the many doors I've had to open in Italian have flung wide, giving onto a sweeping, splendid view. The Italian language did not simply change my life; it gave me a second life, an extra life.

Reading, writing, and living in Italian, I feel like a reader, a writer, a person who is more attentive, active, and curious. Each new word encountered, learned, and listed in my notebook constitutes a small door. My Italian dictionary, meanwhile, serves as a doorway. I think of the books I read, the sentences I write, and the texts I finish all as doors, along with every conversation with an Italian friend, each occasion to express myself.

Italian, in my opinion, is a door more inclusive than exclusive. Otherwise, it wouldn't have been possible for me to write *In Other Words*. That said, even today, when I write in Italian, I feel guilty for having broken open a door I shouldn't have. This new language has turned me into a burglar. That is the strange effect of the question, *Why do you know, speak, and write in our language?* The use of the possessive adjective, *our*, underlines the fact, banal but painful, that Italian is not mine. The process of writing and publishing a book in Italian involved opening another series of doors: all the people with whom I worked, discussed, corrected, and cleaned up the text. I asked of each

---

[2] "perché Romolo, nel tracciare le mura della città con un aratro, lo sollevava proprio nel luogo dove sarebbero state costruite le porte." *Dizionario etimologico* (Santarcangelo di Romagna: Rusconi Libri, 2012).

person, *May I write this sentence, use these words, combine them like this?* That is: *May I cross the border between me and Italian? May I come in?*

After the book was published, the doors that stood before me were my readers. It was their turn to open the cover, to read it. Some would accept my words, some would welcome me. Others, not. This uncertain destiny, for any book, is normal, even right. Each volume, once published, written in whatever language, finds itself on this threshold. To read means, literally, to open a book, and at the same time, to open a part of one's self.

I don't wish to live, or write, in a world without doors. An unconditional opening, without complications or obstacles, doesn't stimulate me. Such a landscape, without closed spaces, without secrets, without the presence of the unknown, would have no significance or enchantment for me.

* * *

The second metaphor I'd like to speak about was also born thanks to Lalla Romano—not from her first book, but from her last. The volume, entitled *Diario ultimo* [Last diary], is a posthumous collection of thoughts, notes, and memories Romano composed in the last years of her life, when she was nearly blind. She annotated large, white sheets of paper in an almost illegible handwriting. I knew nothing about this text, nor about her blindness. The book was given to me in Milan, in the author's home, by Antonio Ria. I was sitting in Romano's living room, surrounded by her library and her paintings. When I learned that she had written a book as she was losing her vision, I felt even closer to her.

Last Diary, an intimate, fragmentary text, is a powerful testimony about the necessity of expressing and identifying oneself through words, and the need to cross a line. Romano writes, with limited eyesight, in a way that is even more lapidary and transparent. Her vision, which turned compromised and approximate, nevertheless blazes with acuity.

I already knew that writing in a new language resembled a sort of blindness. For to write is nothing other than to perceive, observe, and visualize the world. By now I can see in Italian, but only partially. I still grope around in semi-obscurity. Like Romano, I write with an uncertain hand.

The revelation of *Last Diary* is the new perspective that blindness confers. Until I read that book, I asked forgiveness, from my readers and myself, for the limited nature of my Italian. Then Romano enlightened me:

"my near blindness = a point of view"[3]

This was the response I was looking for, ever since I'd started writing in Italian, and felt the need to justify my choice. Romano's succinct statement presents itself like a formula, a theorem. It makes me understand, and appreciate, that the inability to see clearly and fully can illuminate the world in a different way. Despite the distance, it can permit me to strike at the heart of things.

I agree with Romano when she says, "blindness does not prevent me from thinking; in fact, it is a stimulus."[4] I, like her, "do not see what I write."[5] As I've explained in *In Other Words*, I'm still not entirely capable of evaluating my writing in Italian;

---

[3] "la mia quasi cecità = un punto di vista," p. 16.

[4] "La cecità non mi impedisce di pensare, anzi è uno stimolo," p. 69.

[5] "non vedo quello che scrivo," p. 106.

therefore, I remain partly blind to the result. And yet, blindness has made me more vigilant, more agile. Nothing came to me naturally; I had to pay my dues. I understand Romano when she writes: "In the margins one finds possibilities."[6]

Paradoxically, I believe I'm blind even in English, only in reverse. Familiarity, dexterity, and ease with a language can confer another form of blindness. One tends to feel safe, and thus more passive, perhaps even lazy. I can write in English without straining as I must in Italian, without having to examine and double-check almost every word.

It's necessary to clarify that Romano's blindness was a form of physical suffering, while my own is a figurative condition. It remains a creative game and a privilege. And while her infirmity grew progressively worse, I, with time, with experience, am able to see more clearly.

When I first started to write in Italian, I didn't want to conceal the effects of my reduced perception. I didn't want to iron out the text too much, and give the reader the illusion of a vision I lacked. If that had been the goal, I would have continued to write in English. I was aware that the constraints of my Italian annoyed some readers. It can be frustrating to listen to someone who lacks full competence in a language. *Why Italian?* In order to develop another pair of eyes, in order to experiment with weakness.

* * *

The last metaphor is a word that I discovered while reading *La figlia oscura* (translated as *The Lost Daughter*), the third novel by Elena Ferrante, published in 2006. Ferrante is one of the

---

[6] "Nei margini si trovano le possibilità," p. 122.

first Italian authors whom I read directly in Italian, before I moved to Italy, and whom I was able to understand well. Back then, few people outside Italy had heard of her or read her. I was struck by her frank and powerful voice, her unsettling themes, her female characters. I admired her impressive vocabulary thanks to which, I hoped, mine would grow as well.

Among the words that I underlined while reading *The Lost Daughter* was *innesto,* meaning "graft." The protagonist of this short novel is a mother who has a complicated and conflictual relationship with her two daughters. At one point she abandons them, then returns. This woman is disturbed by certain unpleasant traits in her daughter, by the genetic deviation she perceived between them and her. Ferrante writes:

> Even when I recognized in the two girls what I considered my own good qualities I felt that something wasn't right. I had the impression that they didn't know how to make good use of those qualities, that the best part of me ended up in their bodies as a mistaken graft, a parody, and I was angry, ashamed.[7]

Reading the text, I inferred the meaning of *innesto*, but I checked the dictionary all the same. I already knew the term in English: *graft*. But I didn't know the Italian equivalent. I probably would not have been so struck by it had I not found it in Ferrante's novel. She doesn't talk about a successful graft,

---

[7] From Elena Ferrante's *The Lost Daughter*, translated by Ann Goldstein. The Italian original reads, "Anche quando riconoscevo nelle due ragazze quelle che consideravo le mie qualità, sentivo che qualcosa non funzionava. Avevo l'impressione che non sapessero farne un buon uso, che la parte migliore di me, nei loro corpi risultasse un innesto sbagliato, una parodia, e mi arrabbiavo, mi vergognavo," p. 60.

but a graft gone wrong: an imperfect joint, a failure. This is the final metaphor for *In Other Words*, I'd say the one that is most capacious and comprehensive.

Before commenting on the concept of graft, I would like to further explore the definition and connotations of this word.

A botanical term, it describes a system of propagation, an operation through which one obtains better fruit, or a new variety. A graft engenders something original, hybrid. It can be exploited to correct developmental defects—that is, to improve a species, to make it stronger, more resistant.

A graft is an act of insertion. It introduces one element into another. In order to succeed, it presupposes an affinity between the elements at play. It requires connection, fusion, welding. It implies joining one thing to another.

Because it's a transplant, a graft necessitates a displacement, a cut. It results, ideally, in a transformation that feels magical.

This magnificent word, impregnated with psychological, political, and creative nuances, describes my experiment in Italian.

It seems that my decision to write in Italian has emerged from nothing. But this isn't true. My life is a series of grafts, one after the other.

As the child of immigrants, I am myself the fruit of a risky graft that is geographical and cultural. I've been writing from the very beginning about this theme, experience, and trauma. This is how I read the world. A graft explains and defines me. And now that I write in Italian, I myself have become a graft.

I am now trying, as a writer, to graft myself onto a new language. I am aware of the fissure between me and Italian, and of the operation that I've performed up to now, through my writing, in order to bind it.

Like Ferrante's tormented mother, I still fear that the fruit of my graft will go wrong.

But a language, even a foreign language, is something so intimate that it enters inside of us despite the fissure. It becomes a part of our body, our soul. It takes root in the brain, it emerges from our mouths. In time, it nestles in the heart. The graft that I've made puts a new language into circulation, instills new thoughts within me.

This word allows me to move forward, but also narrates my past, my point of origin, my trajectory. It defines the new Italian journey, but also sheds light on my previous writings in English. It was in English that I wrote a book in which the protagonist changes his name. I've been telling stories all along about characters who change country, who transform their reality. A foreigner who arrives from abroad, who learns a new language, who works to contribute to a new society, who integrates herself: this person embodies the word *graft*.

The notion of "graft" helps us to understand a human, universal impulse. It explains why each one of us searches for something else, something more, and it explains how we go about obtaining it. We can change our city, citizenship, body, face, gender, family, religion. Through grafting, we can refute our origins, today more than ever.

Although a graft is a natural process, it can be perceived as forced or inauthentic. Those who undergo or enact it (even on themselves) may be viewed with suspicion.

In order to move forward, to develop as a society, a civilization, it's crucial to change the source of nourishment. I'll recite words of Nathaniel Hawthorne, which serve as the epigraph to my story collection *Unaccustomed Earth*: "Human nature will not flourish, any more than a potato, if it be planted and replanted, for too long a series of generations, in the same worn-out soil." A language, a person, a country: everything is renewed only thanks to contact, closeness, and mixing with the other.

I continue to admit that Italian is not my language, that it's an adopted language I love and use without possession. But I also ask myself: Who possesses a language, and why? Is it a question of lineage? Mastery? Use? Affect? Attachment? What does it mean, in the end, to belong to a language?

A graft can save a life, but the first phase of the process, characterized by fragility, is full of uncertainty. It can go poorly, and the fruit can be nonexistent or bitter. It's always a risky procedure. One needs to have faith and patience, one needs to hope that things will turn out well. Hope that, with time, a new branch will grow. In my case, as a writer and as a person, I seek to grow a new variety of myself.

Now that I'm grafted onto Italian, I still worry. I do all I can to reinforce the connection. This is why I continue to read dictionaries every day, to list new words in my notebook, to interrupt a friend if I hear a term that I don't recognize. This is why I'm afraid of losing contact with Italy. I fear that if the graft is not sufficiently secure, it will rupture.

I remain conscious of the procedure within me: the fusion of the preceding life with the current one, the juncture between the past and the future. Right or wrong, success or failure, the graft persists.

Why Italian? I'd sum it up this way: to open doors, to see differently, to graft myself onto another.

ROME, 2015

Translated by Molly L. O'Brien
in collaboration with the author

(2)

Containers

Introduction to Ties *by
Domenico Starnone*

The need to contain and the need to set free: these are the contradictory impulses, the positive and negative charges that interact in Domenico Scarnone's novel *Ties*. To contain, in Italian, is *contenere*, from the Latin verb *continere*. It means to hold, but it also means to hold back, repress, limit, control. In English, too, we strive to contain our anger, our amusement, our curiosity.

A container is designed so that something can be placed inside it. It has a double identity in that it is either lacking contents or occupied: either empty or full. Containers often hold what is precious. They house our secrets. They keep us safe but can also imprison, ensnare. Ideally, containers stem chaos: they are supposed to keep things from dispersing, disappearing. *Ties* is a novel full of containers, both literal and symbolic. In spite of them, things go missing.

The characters in *Ties* are few: a family of four, a neighbor, a lover who remains offstage. A cat, a carabiniere, a couple of strangers. But there are a number of inanimate objects that also play critical roles in the alchemy of this novel: a swollen envelope that holds a bundle of letters, a hollow cube. Photographs, a dictionary, shoelaces, a home. And what do these objects represent, if not agents of enclosure of various kinds? Envelopes hold letters, and letters contain one's innermost thoughts. Photos contain time, a home contains a family. A hollow cube can contain whatever we'd like it to. A dictionary contains words. Laces—the literal translation of the Italian title, *Lacci*—serve to close up our shoes, which in turn contain our feet.

And as these objects are opened one by one—once the elastic around the envelope is removed, once laces are untied—the novel ignites. Like Pandora's box, each of these objects unleashes acute forms of suffering: frustration, humiliation, yearning, jealousy, envy, rage.

If the myth of Pandora is the leitmotif of *Ties*, Chinese boxes are the underlying mechanism, the morphology. The entire structure of this novel, in fact, seems to me a series of Chinese boxes, one element of the plot discretely and impeccably nestled within the next. There is no hole in the construction, no fissure. No detail has escaped the author's attention; like the home of Aldo and Vanda—the husband and wife at the center of this fleet tale—everything is in place, neat as a pin.

In spite of this airtight structure, the effect is exactly the opposite. A volcanic energy erupts, circulates, spills over in these pages. The novel reckons with messy, uncontrollable urges that threaten to break apart what we hold sacred. It is, in fact, about what happens when structures—social, familial, ideological, mental, physical—fall apart. It asks why we go out of our way to create structures if only to resent them, to evade them, to dismantle them in the end. It is about our collective, primordial need for order, and about our horror, just as primordial, of closed spaces.

Chinese boxes are of course an established narrative device to describe a story that is artfully contained within another story: examples include Tomasi di Lampedusa's short story "The Siren," Mary Shelley's *Frankenstein*. *Ties* plays whimsically with this conceit. It is one novel but it is also several. Though the elements are precisely aligned, though they correspond to one another, they are also severed. One can read the novel as three panels of a triptych, but the image of Chinese boxes remains in my opinion more apt, in that it suggests an infinite number of openings and closings, an endless game.

Let's take it a step further and regard the novel itself as a narrative container. I first called *Ties* a Pandora's box, and then a series of Chinese boxes, but it is also a magician's box that enchants us, from which things appear and disappear. The story jumps around, shifting tonally. And though I have just posited that it is an extremely orderly novel, it is also a gloriously messy one. Points of view are distinct but also blur, time leaps back and forth, expanding and contracting. The trajectory is point to point but also elliptical. The effect is coherent but unpredictable, blissfully free of norms.

Starnone's genius is his ability to play constantly both inside and outside the box, now conforming to it, now escaping it. It is this two-pronged illusion that gives the novel such equilibrium, such force. Though perfectly plotted, though utterly satisfying, it is a novel without a formal conclusion. We never see the end of it. There are obvious scenes to come, always more boxes to confront. The finale has been truncated and we are left in suspense. Only a writer with dexterity of the highest order is capable of pulling off a trick like this.

The metaphor of the magician's box leads us to one of the central, recurrent themes in *Ties*: that of being deceived, betrayed. Whether cheated by an anonymous hustler or an errant husband, by a trick of the mind or fortune's whims, characters are repeatedly being duped, hoodwinked, fooled, lied to. Adultery, in this novel, implies both a physical and moral transgression: stepping outside the family home, breaking the bond between husband and wife. Although breaking that bond may entail little more than moving from one enclosure to the next.

In spite of all the solid walls, the reassuring structures we seek out and build around us, there is nowhere, Starnone seems to suggest, to feel safe. Life is what betrays the container, what spills out. Cesare Pavese comes to mind; in his short story "Suicidi" [Suicides] he observes, "La vita è tutto un tradimento"—*All life is a betrayal*. That is to say, time betrays us, people we know and don't know betray us, we betray ourselves by living, by growing old, and, finally, by dying. Starnone complicates Pavese's observation—unpacking it, if you will. *Ties* is less about betrayal than about pain that returns, that resurfaces: in spite of diligent efforts to organize experiences, emotions, memories, they can't be packaged, hidden, repressed, filed away. Fittingly, at one point, there is a dream in these pages—a fecund, indelible image. For dreams both contain and set free the roiling matter of our psyches.

The multiple themes encased in the novel are densely layered. It is a rumination on old age, on the passage of time, on frailty, on solitude. On forms of inheritance: economic, genetic, emotional. It is a book about marriage, about procreation, about parenting, about love. *Love* is a crucial word in *Ties*, a term that is questioned, redefined, shunned, treasured, maligned. At one point Vanda says that love is merely "a container we stick everything into." It is, in essence, a hollow vessel, a placeholder that justifies our behaviors and choices. A notion that consoles us, that cons us more often than not.

In spite of its stormy course, its dark vision, *Ties* points faithfully toward freedom and its corollary, happiness. Be they virtues or privileges, be they considered a crime; freedom and happiness, in this novel, are one and the same: wild states of being that refuse to be domesticated, that cannot be trammeled or curbed. *Ties* looks coldly at the price of freedom and happiness. It both celebrates and castigates Dionysian states of ecstasy, of abandon. And though happiness often involves linking ourselves to other people—in other words, stepping outside the confines of ourselves—it is something, in the final analysis, that characters experience privately, alone.

In opening her box, Pandora lets the evils of the world circulate. Only hope remains inside, still contained. *Ties*, though caustic, though troubling, remains a hopeful novel. It is bathed in light, it contains moments of great tenderness. It is lyrical, agile, energetic. It is also very funny. It is a great work of literature. And nothing gives me more hope than this.

* * *

As the translator of *Ties* into English, I too have had to break open a formidable container: the container of Italian. For many years I have searched within that box, trying to piece together a new sense of myself. My relationship to Italian incubates and evolves in a sacred vessel I hold dear. My impulse has been to guard it, to not contaminate it.

Then I read *Lacci* when it was published in Italy, in the autumn of 2014, and fell in love with it. I had not yet translated anything from Italian to English. In fact, I was resistant to the idea I was immersed in Italian, in a joyous state of self-exile from the language (English) and the country (the United States) that have marked me most significantly. But the impact of this novel overwhelmed me, and my desire, as soon as I read it, was to translate it someday.

I identified strongly with Aldo because, like him, I had run away, in my case to Italy, taking refuge in the Italian language in search of freedom and happiness. I found them there. Then, like Aldo, after some euphoric years away, with certain misgivings, I decided to return. I moved back to the city that had once been home, where I was surrounded by the language I had deliberately stepped away from. I did all this with a broken heart.

The month after I returned to the United States, *Lacci* won the Bridge Prize for fiction, awarded each year to a contemporary Italian novel or story collection that will be translated into English, and to an American work of fiction that will be translated into Italian. I read the novel for a second time, even more moved by it, and then I discussed it with the author at a panel at the Italian Embassy in Washington, DC. Following the event, Starnone asked if I would consider translating it. I said yes. As a result, this novel has accompanied me during a particularly challenging year of my life. Incidentally, much of it was translated as I was packing up my home, putting everything I have accumulated in my life into a series of boxes.

As a translator I remain outside the container, in that the novel remains the brainchild of a fellow writer. It is liberating in that I don't have to fabricate anything. But I am bound to a preexisting text, and thus aware of a greater sense of responsibility. There is nothing to invent but everything to get right. There is the challenge of transplanting into a different language what already thrives, beautifully, in another. In order to translate *Lacci* I had to purposefully distance myself from Italian, the language I have come to love most, dismantling it, rendering it invisible.

In Starnone's novel, life has to be reread in order to be fully experienced. Only when things are reread, reexamined, revisited, are they understood: letters, photos, words in dictionaries. Translation, too, is a processing of going back over things again and again, of scavenging and intuiting the meaning, in this case multivalent, of a text. The more I read this novel, the more I discovered.

I was struck, as I translated, by a fertile lexicon of Italian terms that mean or describe a state of disorder. I made a list of them: *a soqquadro, devastazione, caos, disordine. Sfasciato, squinternato, divelto, sfregiato. Scempio, disastro, buttare per aria.* These terms are stemmed by a single, prevailing, recurrent word: *ordine.* Order. Or perhaps it is order that is constantly under threat, the terms for disaster engulfing it, undermining it.

Another word that stood out to me, that is used frequently, is *scontento.* It can mean unhappiness in English, but it is far stronger than that. It is an amalgam of frustration, dissatisfaction, disappointment, discontent. And though the roots are different, I couldn't help but ponder the proximity, the interplay between certain verbs in Italian that sound or look similar, that are thematically linked: *contenere* (to contain) and *contentare* (to make happy). *Allacciare* (to lace, tie down) and *lasciare* (to leave).

As I've already noted, *Lacci*, the title of this novel in Italian, means shoelaces. We see them on the cover, thanks to an illustration chosen by the author himself. A person, presumably a man, wears a pair of shoes whose laces are tied together. It is a knot that will surely trip him up, that will get him nowhere. We don't see the expression on the man's face, in fact we see very little of his body. And yet we fear for him, feel a little sorry for him, perhaps laugh at him, given that he already seems to be in the act of falling on his face.

But *lacci* in Italian are also a means of bridling, of capturing something. They connote both an amorous link and a restraining device. "Ties" in English straddles these plural meanings. "Laces" would not have. Having made this choice, I am struck by the relationship in English, too, between *untie* and *unite*, two opposing actions counterpoised in this novel.

What happens when laces are untied? Indeed, as I have already argued, the entire novel is a series of tying and untying, of putting in order and pulling apart, of creating and destroying. "Writing is more about destroying than creating," Karl Ove Knausgård has observed. There is some truth to this. But art is nothing if not contained by a unique structure, held in place by an inviolable unique form.

My American friend and fellow translator from Italian Michael Moore, believes that Starnone—a Neapolitan writer who grew up speaking dialect, who learned to write in Italian, as so many Italian writers do—is one of the few contemporary Italian authors today who writes in an uncontaminated Italian. My Italian writer friends, too, hail his transparent, nuanced, erudite prose. I agree with them. Starnone's rhythm and lexicon float free from any trend. His style is protean. His sentences can be lapidary but others are intricate, centripetal, revealing a subtle inlay of clauses—Chinese boxes on the syntactical level. In translating them I have often had to rupture their design, restructuring in order to render them at home in English. His prose is steeped in classical allusions, psychoanalytic references, the laws of physics. This novel, his thirteenth work of fiction, fits into no distinct category or genre: it is a clever whodunit, a comedy of errors, a domestic drama, a tragedy. It is an astute commentary on the sexual revolution, on women's liberation, on rational and irrational urges. It is like a cube, perfectly proportioned; turn it around, and you will discover another facet.

There is a passage in this novel that stopped me in my tracks the first time I encountered it, that moves me in particular each time I reread it. It involves a writer alone in his study, not writing but, rather, sorting through his books and papers. It is a meditation on existence and on identity in its most essential form, and it helps me to understand the impetus behind what I myself do. It is a passage about leaving traces, about trying desperately, in vain, to tie ourselves to life itself. It lays bare the flawed human impulse to endure.

Writing is a way to salvage life, to give it form and meaning. It exposes what we have hidden, unearths what we have neglected, misremembered, denied. It is a method of capturing, of pinning down, but it is also a form of truth, of liberation.

If one is to unpack all the boxes, this is a novel, I believe, about language, about storytelling and its discontents. The disquieting message of *Ties* is not so much that life is fleeting, that we are alone in this world, that we hurt one another, that we grow old and forget, but that none of this can be captured, not even by means of literature. Containers may be the destiny of many in that they hold our remains after death. But this novel reminds us that narrative refuses to stay put, and that the effort of telling stories only pins things down so far. In the end it is language itself that is the most problematic container; it holds too much and too little at the same time.

I am deeply grateful to Domenico Starnone not only for the work he has produced but for inviting me and trusting me to translate it. It is with *Lacci* that I return to English after a hiatus of not working with the language for nearly four years. It is this project that has inspired me to reopen my English dictionaries, my old thesaurus, after a considerable period of neglect. My fear, before I began, was that it would distance me from Italian, but the effect has been quite the contrary. If anything, I feel more tied to it than ever. I have encountered countless new words, new idioms, new ways of phrasing things. And though I translated the book in America, it has also brought me closer in some sense to Rome, the city in which I was living when I discovered the book, the city in which much of the novel's action is set. It is in Rome, the city to which I will forever hap-pily return, that I revised and completed the translation, and where I write these words of introduction.

These scattered observations cannot possibly contain my admiration for what Domenico Starnone has achieved in these pages. I am tempted to better organize my thoughts, but all I really want to say is: open his book. Read it, reread it. Discover the words, the voice, the sleight of hand of this brilliant writer.

ROME, 2016

(3)

Juxtaposition

Introduction to Trick *by*
Domenico Starnone

Dolcetto o scherzetto is Italian for "trick or treat," only inverted: the literal translation is *treat or trick*. A prankster's slogan that masked children, seeking something sweet, say in the dark, in a darkening season, on the thresholds of strangers' homes. The phrase, coined in America, is both solicitous and imperative, mirthful and menacing. When a child says "trick or treat" on Halloween night, it's up to the adult either to play along or suffer the consequences.

And so I landed on *Trick* as an English title for *Scherzetto*, Domenico Starnone's fourteenth novel, even though Halloween has relatively little traction in Italy, and has nothing to do with this book. But when I translated the word *scherzetto* in one of the novel's key scenes, *trick* fell short. My spontaneous solution was the expression *gotcha*, and after completing the first draft, I asked Starnone if the Italian equivalent (*ti ho beccato*) conveyed the sense of *scherzetto*. Not really, he replied, adding that it was closer to a proposal: "Let's play around, let's have a little fun."

The adjective *little* is key; *scherzetto* is the diminutive of the noun *scherzo*, derived from the verb *scherzare*, which means, principally, to joke or to play. *Scherzi*, one quips in Italian to say, *you're kidding*. Musicians know that *scherzo* indicates a vigorous movement in a composition, to be executed playfully. Note the associative, connective tissue rapidly forming between these words: *trick, joke, kid, kidding, play*.

Trick is an extremely playful literary composition. It's about a kid, dealing with a kid, having kids, kidding around. It's about how it feels when the joke's on you. In some sense, the real protagonist of this novel is not a person but a playing card: the Joker. A trump card, a wild card, a jester, a clown. A card of American origin whose identity is mutable, that can substitute for others. One might think that the word for Joker in Italian would have something to do with *scherzo*. Instead it's called a *jolly*, an English adjective that has become an Italian noun, the imported etymology based on the fact that early versions of the card were called the Jolly Joker.

Borrowing, copying, converting, replacing, bleeding toge-ther: *Trick* is an ongoing act of juxtaposition, a thrust and parry in which two very different works of fiction confront, confound, and cross-pollinate one another. *Trick*, set in Naples, is about an aging illustrator commissioned to create images for a deluxe Italian edition of "The Jolly Corner," a celebrated ghost story by Henry James, published in 1908 and set in New York City. James was an American author who spent most of his life in Europe. Starnone is an Italian author, arguably the finest alive in that country today, who has spent considerable time reading Henry James.

The central action of *Trick*, spanning just four days, takes place in November, the darkest of months, and is steeped in gothic references: apparitions, howling winds, figures that disappear down corridors. It is about things that go bump in the night, people who ring doorbells and are not terribly kind. It is about the fear of slipping and falling, of failure, of illness, of facing phantoms, of facing death. Perhaps, in some sense, Halloween does have something to do with it: like a flickering jack-o'-lantern, at once illuminating and terrifying, the whole novel can be read as a dialectic between darkness and light.

Trick makes us grin and at times makes us cackle with laughter, but it also unnerves, settling over us like a damp chill. Much of the discomfort derives from the narrator's ambivalent attitude toward Mario, his four-year-old grandson. Their relationship is always vacillating between affection and antagonism, solidarity and spite. Unlike his grandfather, a convalescent in his seventies tormented by his lack of vitality, Mario represents agility, potential, life in spades. Evolution is an underlying theme of this novel, and thus, survival of the fittest. One can read *Trick* as a domesticated version of *Lord of the Flies*, the island swapped for an apartment in Naples, the repercussions every bit as savage. Grandfather and grandson are marooned together, also pitted apart; both are essentially abandoned by the adult world.

The drama unfolds from the grandfather's point of view. He has a name, Daniele, but it is so seldom mentioned that one tends to overlook it. Mario, on the other hand, commands the spotlight. The child is at once precocious and innocent, unbearable and vulnerable. He can neither read nor tell time and yet he repeatedly outwits a man seven decades his senior. Daniele is a protective, anxious caregiver, but also palpably aggressive, neglectful, and mean. Mario's impulse to mimic his grandfather is poignant, and might be read as a form of flattery, but it is interpreted, by a puerile old man who bristles even at the term *nonno* (grandfather in Italian), as defeat. An epigraph

for *Trick* might have come from Heraclitus: "Time is a child
at play, with his checkers; governance belongs to a child."[1]

Like Mario and his grandfather, the very narrative weave of
this novel is at loggerheads. It shuttles between witty dialogue
and rich meditative passages, fast-paced action and scalding
interior reflection. It is tonally bifurcated, serious and silly, lu-
gubrious and lighthearted, ironic, desperate, full of bile. The
Italian writer Goffredo Fofi points out that it is written in "two
different registers." Conversations between characters are what
push the story forward. But stepping back, the reader discovers
a potent metafictional exchange between *Trick* and "The Jolly
Corner," as well as a series of broader analogies between New
York and Naples, James and Starnone, language and image,
present and past.

This novel reminds us that much of art is about communicating with the dead. There is no disputing the fact that *Trick*
resembles—one might go so far as to say channels—"The Jolly
Corner." Not surprisingly, both works are preoccupied by notions of similitude, simulacra, doubles, interchangeability. At
first glance, the surprising kinship, independently forged by
Starnone, seems straightforward: both stories, simply put, are
about the horror of returning to one's place of origin. But a

---

[1] "αἰὼν παῖς ἐστι παίζων, πεσσεύων· παιδὸς ἡ βασιληίη": fragment B52. I am
grateful to Barbara Graziosi for the English translation of this fragment.
I include an alternative translation, by William R. Dingee: "Life is a
child at play, a game of checkers; the throne belongs to the child." Dingee
comments: "It would be nice to preserve the etymological link in παῖς
παίζων—literally a 'child child-ing, a child being a child' but I'm not
sure I know how." He adds, "The word αἰών generally means the time of
a life, a lifespan, or else a long period of time: age, epoch (eon being a
derivative), or even 'eternity.' I translated 'life' meaning life regarded as a
period of time (as opposed to *bios*, *zoë*, life as a biological phenomenon, or *chronos*, a more unmarked term for time)."

close reading of these texts—and I highly recommend this—
yields innumerable, more subtle points of contact: echoes,
clues, inside jokes. True, the text of James's story hasn't been
inserted between the covers of *Trick*, and Starnone's novel can
be fully appreciated without reading a word of James. It would
be a pity, though.

In addition to riffing consummately on "The Jolly Corner,"
Trick resuscitates James's work and themes more generally. I
could not help but think of *Washington Square* (both works de-
pict a charged father-daughter relationship and a problematic
son-in-law figure); "The Turn of the Screw" (his most famous
ghost story, about a frazzled adult left alone with a precocious
child); "The Real Thing" (narrated by an illustrator, and all
about the dichotomy between reality and representation); and
"The Figure in the Carpet" (about a widowed husband, and a
wife's secrets).

The convergence with James reaches its apogee, however,
in the appendix to *Trick*, a sort of free-associating, illustrated
artist's diary, tonally divergent, which glosses the main story
and also distills its essence. The appendix reverses gear, the
entries spanning the weeks leading up to the novel's action.
Drawings crowd the margins, both enhancing and crowding
out the words. The appendix is an organ literally cut out of the
story, seemingly extraneous but in fact fundamental to our understanding: an intimate commentary and also a tour de force
in which sentences from James's story, in Italian translation,
have been ingeniously spliced into the text. So, while Starnone
and James remain separate authors of separate works of fiction, the appendix, itself a hybrid piece of writing, fuses them
together. *Trick* is no mere homage to James; it is a willful act of
combining, of appropriation, of grafting, on both a thematic
and linguistic plane.

Italy's love affair with American literature begins more or less around the time of Starnone's birth, in 1943, which coincides with the fall of Fascism. James was among the thirty-three largely unknown American authors translated for the first time in *Americana*, an anthology edited by Elio Vittorini, published in 1941, that profoundly influenced postwar Italian writing. Vittorini extolled Hemingway; Cesare Pavese famously translated *Moby-Dick*. These writers did more than love American literature; they identified with it, drew hope and vitality from it. What Starnone does in *Trick*, more than seven decades after *Americana*, takes this love affair to new extremes and renders an Italian writer's identification with an American novelist textually specific.

James is the obvious frame of reference, but there is another literary key I feel compelled to mention: Kafka. For *Trick* explores themes and preoccupations central to Kafka's vision. One, surely, is an obsession with the body: with physical discomfort, with weakness, with disease. The tragicomic description of an old man struggling to get out of bed in the morning on the first page of *Trick* reminded me of Gregor Samsa's immediate predicament following his metamorphosis. Mario's bound-less physical prowess—he is always jumping, moving around, doing things—only exacerbates Daniele's sense of feeling debilitated, constrained. Much of their friction can be summed up as a contrast between bodies: one small and mighty, the other large, laid low.

Kafka, like the narrator of *Trick*, had an aversion toward children. Elias Canetti observes, "Thus it is really envy that Kafka feels in the presence of children, but envy of a kind different from that which might be expected: an envy coupled with disapproval."[2] *Trick* is very much about envy: generational,

---

[2] Canetti, p. 36.

professional, sexual. Like the narrator of *Trick*, Kafka detested his father. The compressed, recondite appendix recalls the sensibility of Kafka's own *Diaries*, a heterodox merging of observation and storytelling. And, finally: *Trick* shares, with Kafka, and with James for that matter, a charged relationship to physical space, and the frequent need for open air. Most of *Trick*'s action is set indoors, or on thresholds. The tension between inside and outside is ongoing, similar to the play between darkness and light. But the most memorable scene of the novel takes place on a balcony: a platform perched over nothing, a space that plays with space itself.

The balcony, in *Trick*, is a locus of risk and of refuge, of exile as well as freedom. It is a rejection of family and origins, and also reeks of those very origins. It is a place where one is permitted to see beyond, to project. The balcony represents the precarious state of everything: youth, fame, relationships, life itself. Anything can break off, plummet at a moment's notice. This existential anxiety is the mass of air upon which the novel paradoxically rests. The void represents emptiness, death, but also creation. For this is the artist's habitat: turned away from a secure foundation, creating from nothing.

There are extraordinary passages in this novel about what it means to become an artist, about the mechanics and mystery of inspiration. It describes what happens when an artist begins to slow down, struggle, question his own production. Making art is a form of playing, a game the artist plays for tremendous stakes. Starnone plays with James; perhaps he is also playing with Kafka, an author, along with Calvino, whom he often cites as a literary forefather. Calvino played vigorously with his reader, his characters, with genre, with the essence of narrative itself, as did Pirandello, Svevo, and Nabokov. Starnone is a player on this team.

An attentive reader of Starnone will find further interplay among his previous works. Certainly *Spavento* (a novel largely about illness, whose title means fear in Italian), *Via Gemito* (about childhood in Naples, about a hateful and hated father), and *Ties* (about defining ourselves, growing older, and what binds one generation to the next). *Trick* stems from this body of work but is its own creature, inventive at its very core. Of course, this is all speculation on my part. Starnone is a writer who knows never to show his full hand.

The underlying theme, visited again and again in Starnone, is identity. Who are we, where and what do we come from, why do we become what we become? In *Trick*, more succinctly than ever, he examines heredity, the effects of coupling, what is handed down, what slips through the cracks. Identity, for Starnone, is never singular but multiple, never static, always in flux. Identity entails selection, assortment, happenstance, strategy, risk. This is why the principal metaphor in *Trick* is a deck of cards, which spawns the act of discarding: shunning possibilities, setting them aside, whittling down options in order to shape ourselves, our futures. Not surprisingly, the novel pays special attention to adolescence, a phase in which a child's body is violently reacting, expanding, and altering itself, a phase at the end of which we are expected to choose our path and become an adult. The novel confronts the tension between what lies in the cards and the consequence of playing the cards we're dealt. What ultimately haunts is the hypothetical (a conditional construction particularly dear to Italian grammar, and consciousness): what one might have been, how things might have turned out. Like Spencer Brydon in "The Jolly Corner," the protagonist of *Trick* is assaulted less by who he's become than by what he didn't; by what James calls "all the old baffled foresworn possibilities."

The word *scherzetto* also means "a minor work or composition" in Italian. But there is nothing minor about this novel apart from Mario, who is indeed quite small. *Trick* is not a story for children, nor is it a novel for those in need of reassurance. Here is the fine print that most of us prefer to ignore as we blunder through life. It warns us that childhood is scary, as is falling in love and getting married, as is old age. We are prey to rage along the way: at one's parents, one's offspring, one's choices, one's own blood. And there is no escape from fear: of who we really are, of what we see and what we don't.

I translated *Trick* almost exactly one year after translating *Ties*, Starnone's previous novel. In some sense, I had a running start, given that I was already familiar with the author's pacing, tics, and fixations. But *Trick* was trickier. The title remains a compromise, only a partial solution. This novel also contains Neapolitan dialect, new territory for me. The use of dialect underscores the tonal double register, and also represents the protagonist's hostile relationship to himself, his city of origin, his past. Some of this dialect I intuited. Other terms, rife with violence and obscenity, were politely translated for me into Italian by Starnone himself.

Certain wordplay was impossible to capture. What to do, for example, with a term like *schizzar via*? It appears in a passage which describes the balcony, and is used to convey the tenuous connection between a building and the cantilevered platform that protrudes. I translated it as "flying off." But *schizzare* refers to liquids, too. It's the water flicked between Mario and his grandfather when they say "*scherzetto*" to each other (though, in that scene, Starnone opts for a close cousin, *spruzzare*). *Schizzare* refers to fluids that burst, that hemorrhage. In the opening paragraph, we learn that the artist-protagonist of *Scherzetto* has undergone surgery followed by blood loss, a transfusion.

Serendipitously, *schizzo* is also the word for a drawing, a sketch, the first draft of a book.

Trezziare was another dilemma, another delight. It's a strictly Neapolitan verb that refers to the card game *tresette*, and refers to the slow reveal of cards in hopes of finding the "three" that wins the game. But it has a broader meaning in Neapolitan culture, used to describe the sensation of joyfully anticipating something, for example, the way a child counts down to Christmas. It's a word tailor-made for *Trick*, a term that stitches together many of its myriad themes. In Italian, one slowly savors the full range of meaning, of reverberations. In English, much of this linguistic complexity drains away.

To translate is to walk down numerous scary corridors, to grope in the dark. I took my cue from the illustrator-protagonist of *Trick*. In the appendix he writes, "thoroughly knowing the text is the first step to working properly." This was what I did, reading and rereading not just Starnone but James, first in English, then in Italian translation, thereby both closing the circle and forming a triangle. Translation, much like this novel, is the intersection of two texts and voices, but a legitimate translation of *Trick* required three players: Starnone, James, and myself.

Reading "The Jolly Corner" in English after translating *Trick* was something like walking through a hall of mirrors. Sentences, words, images, and motifs began to emerge, recognizable but distorted, and to startle me. *Trick* rewards the reader who looks carefully. Like "The Jolly Corner," it plays with optics, with the eye and with "I." To read both texts is to experience an act of ongoing mutual illumination, each text serving as an annotation and alter ego of the other.

The more I moved between texts the more I marveled. Starnone uses languages the way a great painter works with color, conjuring the illusion of three dimensions from a blank flat surface. I spent days deepening my understanding of key terms in *Trick*: *scherzare*, *giocare*, *buio*, *rabbia*, *vuoto* (joking, playing, darkness, anger, emptiness). When Starnone plays with these words, he knows how to tease out and release their potential, how to shuffle their complex ontological identities, in brief, how to *trezziare* with unparalleled finesse.

Scholars and critics will be playing for years with this novel, exploring its various layers, links, correspondences. As a translator, I, too, had my share of fun. My version of *Trick*, the first in English, is just one of many that might have been. A translation is nothing if not a process of elimination. For every sentence I constructed, I had to discard numerous possibilities. A translation is also, by definition, the offshoot of a preexisting text. My hope, immodest as it will sound, was to channel Starnone's style, to write as if he were writing, to somehow copy-and-paste him into English. This, too, involves something of a trick. A translation surgically alters the text's identity, insisting upon a foreign linguistic DNA, requiring a transfusion of alternate grammar and syntax. The generational bond between texts is indisputable. One descends from the other, and thus they remain connected, as distinct as they may be. Translation is an act of doubling and converting, and the resulting transformation is precarious, debatable even in its final form. Starnone's text remains the parent that spawned this translation, but somewhere along the road to its English incarnation, it also became a ghost.

PRINCETON, 2016

(4)

In Praise of Echo

*Reflections on the Meaning
of Translation*

In February of 2016, I welcomed a group of students at Princeton University to a seminar dedicated to literary translation. I was eager to teach the course, but even more eager to learn from it myself. For it was precisely during that period that I was about to face my first formal translation project: the novel *Lacci*, written by Domenico Starnone and published in 2014, which I had read in Italian and loved.

The translation of *Lacci* was part of an ongoing phase of metamorphosis in my life. In 2012, I had moved to Rome with the objective of improving my Italian. The following year I began writing in Italian, and this experiment led to *In altre parole*, composed in Italian and published in 2015. I felt bold and adventurous, but in the back of my mind, in bypassing translation, I also felt that I had skipped a crucial step on the path to acquiring and genuinely knowing a new language.

When Starnone, whom I befriended in Rome, proposed that I translate *Lacci*, I accepted with enthusiasm, but also with apprehension. It was one thing for me to undergo a transformation from writing in English to Italian. It would be quite another to transform from a writer of my own novels to a translator of someone else's words. In some sense, the thought of undergoing this second metamorphosis felt more radical than the first. It came with a sense of responsibility I had not previously had to consider. And it required not only skills but a state of mind with which I was less familiar.

In planning the first translation seminar at Princeton, I asked myself how to begin, how best to introduce and open up the conversation. I had read many essays, many theories of translation in the past. I could easily have begun by citing essays by Walter Benjamin or by Vladimir Nabokov. Instead, I turned to Ovid's *Metamorphoses*, a work that never fails to illuminate life's mysteries to me. Let us keep in mind that Ovid's masterpiece is itself a translation, in a broad sense, of Greek mythology, inspired perhaps by the Roman poet's travels to Greece as young man, and his study of the ancient Greek language and culture. Like almost all Latin poetry, the *Metamorphoses* is a work that grows out of an encounter with, and rerendering of, a preexisting literature composed in another tongue.[1] Within the poem, I thought immediately of the myth of Echo and Narcissus, and it began to orient me, providing me with certain keys with which to begin exploring what it means to translate a text from one language to another.

---

[1] Glenn W. Most, in discussing the crucial role of translation in Roman culture, includes Ovid in his list of Latin poets who "continued to enrich the resources of the Latin language, to broaden their reader's experience, to refine their own techniques, and to establish a cultural identity for Rome, by translating into Latin whole works, portions, or even just famous quotations from the Greek they read at school," p. 388.

I began, on the first day of class, by saying that all translation must be regarded first and foremost as a metamorphosis: a radical, painful, and miraculous transformation in which specific traits and elements are shed and others are newly obtained. In this sense, I told the class, nearly every episode in Ovid's great narrative poem can be read metaphorically as an example of translation, given that creatures are constantly changing states of being. That said, the myth of Echo and Narcissus is particularly resonant when considered from a translator's point of view, and it speaks to me personally, acutely, about what it means to shift from writer to translator and back again.

Let's begin by refreshing our memory of the myth, found in book 3 of the *Metamorphoses*. A doomed love story, it is one of a series of tales in Ovid in which both the lover and the beloved are transformed. Echo, a mountain nymph known for her sonorous voice, is enlisted by the philandering Zeus to distract Juno by chatting with her. When Juno learns that she has been deceived by Echo's talkative nature, she condemns her to say only a portion of what other people have already said. Her capacity to speak is altered, reduced to a partial repetition of words previously generated by others: "Nevertheless, when chatting, her powers of speech / were no different then than now; that is to say, / she could only repeat, from several words, the very last of them" ("et tamen usum / garrula non alium quam nunc habit oris habebat, / reddere de multis ut uerba nouissima posset," 359–61).

Translation has always been a controversial literary form, and those who are resistant to it or dismiss it complain that the resulting transformation is a "mere echo" of the original— that too much has been lost in the process of traveling from one language into another. Ovid's story draws attention to the nature of this loss, or impoverishment, as personified by Echo, a figure who inspires the word, also Greek in origin, to explain an acoustic phenomenon: a sound that, as a result of moving in a certain way and encountering a barrier, "returns," replicating a portion of the original sound. We must be careful, however, not to equate the word *echo* with simple repetition. The verb Ovid attributed to Echo, once condemned, is not *repetere* but *reddere*, which means, among other things, to restore, to render, to reproduce. It can also mean to translate from one language to another.[2]

At first glance, it seems that Echo, who starts out as a talented storyteller, is converted, thanks to Juno's curse, into a translator. For, like Echo, part of the translator's task is to "listen" to a text by carefully reading it, absorbing its meaning, and repeating it back. The translator reproduces words already written by duplicating them. Like Echo, the translator's art presupposes the existence of an original text, and also presupposes that much of what makes that text beautiful and unique in the original will be impossible to maintain in another linguistic context. In Ovid's myth, Echo's condition is clearly a punishment, a deprivation of her own voice and words. But she who translates, ideally, converts this "punishment" into a stimulating challenge, and often a joy. The translator "repeats" and thus "doubles" a text, but this repetition must not be taken literally. Far from a restrictive act of copying, a translator restores the meaning of a text by means of an elaborate, alchemical process that requires imagination, ingenuity, and freedom. And so, while the act of repeating, or echoing, is certainly pertinent to the subject of translation, it is only the starting point of the translator's art.

---

[2] See Cicero, *De Oratore* 1.34.55 ("quae legeram Graece, Latine redderem / I translated into Latin what I had read in Greek") and Ovid, *Tristia* 5.7.53-54 ("unus in hoc nemo est populo, qui forte Latine / quaelibet e medio reddere verba queat. / In this population there is not one who, by chance, is capable of translating even commonplace words into Latin.")

Let's proceed with our myth. Echo, one day, falls in love with Narcissus, and as a result her condition, already compromised, turns tragic. Lacking her own words, she is unable to call out to Narcissus, whom she desires. When she eventually approaches him, he repudiates her, and in a cruel comedy of errors, Narcissus, in the course of resisting her advances, falls in love with himself. Echo, in her shame, wastes away, her body vanishing, to the point where she is nothing but a heap of bones and a voice. Ovid's language is emphatic and haunting: "Only voice and bones survive. / The voice endures; the bones, they say, assumed the look of stones" ("uox tantum atque ossa supersunt: / uox manet; ossa ferunt lapidis traxisse figuram," 398–99). The repetition of the Latin *vox*, voice, celebrates Echo's very curse, acknowledging her original talent. The word, literally echoed, elevates the insubstantial, invisible, but enduring part of her, drawing it paradoxically into sharp relief.

These plot points are charged with meaning from the translator's point of view. Two details are fundamental, and both refer to Echo. First, the act of desiring, of falling in love, which, under ideal circumstances, is what instigates the impulse to translate. Passion, as I said, was what moved me to translate *Lacci*, and everything I have translated since. I have been fortunate thus far to pick and choose my translation projects. There is no better or more satisfying way to satisfy one's love for a text than to translate it. To translate a book is to enter into a relationship with it, to approach and accompany it, to know it intimately, word by word, and to enjoy the comfort of its company in return.

One of the conditions of this relationship is the act of following, of being second and not first. Like Echo, who in Ovid "sees and burns for him, furtively following his tracks" ("uidit et incaluit, sequitur uestigia furtim," 371), a translator comes to know an author's work by literally following its tracks, by pursuing it attentively. Fittingly, we often praise a translator's efforts when we say that he or she has "captured" the spirit and sense of the original. One might say that a figurative hunt is involved, represented not only by the inevitable toil of hunting down the right words to re-create the text, but by a stealthy shadowing—the result of countless readings and reflections upon the work itself—in order to best understand its form, its structure, its meaning. Ironically, Echo—in one of the many surprising role reversals in this myth—is the principal hunter, while Narcissus, who is described as a hunter, is the one, for the most part, running away. Though Echo's hunt ends in failure, she helps us to better appreciate the translator's contradictory role as someone who both comes second and exercises a certain degree of power in the course of wrestling a text into a new language.

I would like to pause for a moment on the ramifications of being first as opposed to second. Now that I have become a translator in addition to remaining a writer, I am struck by how many people regard what I am doing as "secondary" and thus creatively inferior in nature. Translation, it seems, is considered imitative as opposed to imaginative. Some people, when I tell them I am translating someone else's work as opposed to writing something of my own, appear almost sorry for me, as if translation projects represent a dearth of my own ideas, the solution for a fallow period, a drying up of my original voice. Readers who react with suspicion to a work in translation reinforce a perceived hierarchy in literature between an original work and its imitation. This hierarchy, sadly prevalent, between what is authentic and what is derivative—one might take another step and say, between what is pure and what is tainted—influences not only how we regard literature but how we regard one another. Who is original, who belongs authentically to a place? Who does not? Why are those who are not original to a place—migrants who did not "get there first"—treated as they are? I will turn to these implications further ahead. For now, let's return to our myth and to translation.

The second salient point regards Echo in her final "incarnation," as it were, as nothing but a voice. Translators are often described as being invisible, discreet, self-sacrificing presences. Their names are frequently absent on book covers; their roles are meant to be supportive. Once the book has been translated, they are expected to erase themselves out of the picture and allow the book to speak for itself. Indeed, feminist scholars have argued that the practice of translation corresponds to traditional feminine archetypes in which a woman's position and identity were subservient to a man's. Echo's wasting away, her loss of flesh, also brings to mind the penitential practices of medieval saints.

In a span of three years, I translated both *Lacci* and *Scherzetto* by Starnone. On both occasions, I wrote introductions that expressed my admiration and critical appreciation of Starnone's works, with the exclusive aim of presenting him to a new readership. For my efforts I was chastised by critics, more than once, for interfering with the reader's relationship with the book, for drawing attention to my own thoughts, and for casting light upon my role as translator. One reviewer (both were men) pointed to my introduction as an example of "energy-sapping intellectualization." Another's advice: "Maybe next time, Lahiri could just skip the introduction and let Starnone do all the talking."

Like Echo before she is cursed, I was made to feel that I had been loquacious. I have no interest, here, in defending myself. What I find relevant is the ongoing desire to render the translator innocuous and unobtrusive. After being rejected by Narcissus, Echo turns physically absent: "Ever since, she lurks in the woods and is spotted on no mountain" ("inde latet siluis nulloque in monte videtur," 400). The very next line, however, reads: "She is heard by all: sound is what lives of her" ("omnibus auditor: sonus est qui uiuit in illa," 401). Her invisibility is countered and compensated for by the presence of her voice. Again she is a contradiction, nowhere to be seen, always to be heard. How should translators, who strive to echo works of literature on their own linguistic terms, according to their vision and interpretation of it, strike a balance?

Let's now turn to Narcissus, who shares center stage in this myth, and who has spawned an adjective that has come to represent an all-too-common aspect of human psychology. As previously mentioned, Narcissus is described by Ovid as a hunter, proud and independent, conforming to conventional notions of what a writer is: a singular, inimitable voice, to be doubled and diffused, perhaps, by a translator's echo. If we are now to draw a two-part analogy in which Echo represents the translator and, by properties of synecdoche, also a work in translation, then Narcissus personifies the writer, and also the original text.

The circumstances of Narcissus are intriguing from the start. The seer Tiresias warns his mother, Liriope, that in order to grow old, he must lack self-knowledge: "If he does not know himself" / "si se non nouerit" (348). This cryptic warning, the opposite of the legendary inscription in Delphi to "know oneself" (in Greek, γνῶθι σεαυτόν / *gnōthi seauton*) disturbs and fascinates, and also rings true. I speak from personal experience. It is imperative for me to know a text in order to translate it: I must know not only what it means, but how it comes to mean what it means. As a writer, caught up in the act of writing, I am far more ignorant, and even unconscious, of what I do. The heady self-involvement of writing can be at odds with a more distanced perspective. Writing, like Narcissus's conviction that the image he sees in the pond is someone other than himself, corresponds at times to a quite infantile state in which objective reason has little to no relevance. Even afterward, I can try to explain what something I have written means, but in the end I am only explaining from within myself, from my limited point of view.

Narcissus is tricked by the illusion that the beautiful boy he sees reflected in the pool is someone other than himself. But, in building up my analogy, I wonder if my lesson on translation is also somewhat deceiving. Echo represents certain traits of the translator, true, but then so does Narcissus, in that a translation is both an acoustic and visual reflection of a text constituted in other words, something that must be both heard and visualized by the translator, a reflection that "seems" to be the original while in fact being quite separate and distinct. The trick to a good translation is to be unable to recognize which is which. The minute a translation "feels" or "sounds" like a translation, the reader jumps back and accuses it, rejects it. The enormous expectation we place upon translation is that it sound "true." This is why the demands upon a translation are even greater than those placed on an original text.

But what makes something original, as opposed to a derivation? As a writer, I can vouch for the fact that everything "original" I have ever written derives necessarily from something else, not just from my experiences but from my reading of other works, and through inspiration I have drawn, consciously and unconsciously, from countless other authors. Creativity does not exist in a vacuum, and much of it involves responding by imitating, as theorists from Plato to Erich Auerbach to Harold Bloom have reminded us. I am attracted to myths—incidentally, the very first stories I learned to read—not only because they point me back to my own origins as a reader, but because they are the only original stories that exist: stories with counterparts in all cultures that belong to everyone and to no one. When I began writing stories as a child, I wrote copies of what I read, and in many respects, that is what I've have continued doing, in only a slightly less obvious way. The illusion of artistic freedom is just that, an illusion. No words are "my words"—I merely arrange and use them in a certain way.

Echo and Narcissus can be regarded as opposites and, like many opposites, as two sides of the same coin. If we attribute, to Echo, the act of repeating, which comes from the Latin *repetere*, then Narcissus, the hunter, would be aligned with *petere,* meaning to strike, to seek, to assail. On the one hand their dynamic corresponds to a patriarchal model, declined along conventional gender lines. The translation remains at the service of a text, whereas the text, proudly independent, resists being marred, preserved in its original state. Certainly, the text continues to occupy a privileged position: read, unaltered over centuries, intact, in accordance with the author's intentions. While a work of art, however imperfect or incomplete, is regarded as definitive, translation is emphatically the opposite. Translation must continuously adapt to the needs of the present. It cannot divorce itself from the moment at hand, for its goal is to reach readers, to gain a contemporary audience. That is why even the greatest works of translation are always replaced by others. Translations are dispensable, but the truth is that they are also indispensable. The ongoing, updated echo of translation is critical to sustaining great works of literature, to celebrating and spreading their significance across space and time.

Echoes are phenomena, marvelous but also unsettling, even spooky. Let's revisit the climactic scene in the myth, the moment in which Narcissus hears Echo seeking, in vain, to call him. Echo, deprived, as we have already established, of her own voice, wishes to address her beloved, but can only repeat what he says: "What she can do / is prepare to wait for sounds, and send them back in her own words" ("sed, quod sinit, illa parata est / exspectare sonos, ad quos sua uerba remittat," 377–78). Here the Latin *exspectare*, with its combined sense of waiting and longing, merits special attention, underscoring Echo's emotional and vocal condition. And when she repeats, therefore, "There is" ("adest") to his "Is anyone there?" ("ecquis adest?" 380), Narcissus is "dumbstruck" ("hic stupet," 381). As their tangled, tragicomic conversation ensues, Narcissus seeks that voice, and for an instant it is Narcissus who is in pursuit, and Echo who flees him. And so he asks, "Is it me you flee?" ('quid' inquit / 'me fugis?,' 383-84). When Echo advances physically, however, Narcissus again "flees"—("ille fugit," 390)—and in retreating, refuses her touch, going so far as to say that he would rather die than embrace her.

Why is an echo—as we have already established, an act of love, of listening and of restoring—so threatening? Why does that sound, which is in fact our own sound, recast by means of another, undermine and even threaten to annihilate our sense of who we are?

Had the myth of Narcissus and Echo had a happy ending, their child might have grown up to become a writer-translator like me. I can trace aspects of my own creative impulses to both figures. For writing is, among other things, a deep and direct regarding of oneself. The best of writing comes from unflinching introspection. And yet I see myself equally in Echo. From my earliest memories I have been listening to the world, trying to cast back the experiences of others. I may have begun by writing my own books, but I was born with a translator's disposition, in that my overriding desire was to connect disparate worlds. I have devoted a great deal of energy in my life to absorbing the language and culture of others: the Bengali of my parents, and then later, after I became an adult, Italian, a language which I have now creatively adopted. When I write in Italian, one way to perceive it would be as an echo of the language itself. Let's go back to the scientific explanation—what happens when a language, in encountering a foreign body (in this case, me) is cast back differently?

Some Italian readers of my Italian work define it as "my Italian," correct but anomalous, to be kept separate from a more accepted, authentic Italian. It has been suggested to me to be more careful and conservative with my use of the language were I to write in Italian again, so as not to "offend" certain readers. Italian in its official form—whatever that may mean—should not and cannot, according to such readers, be touched or marred. My Italian is considered an echo in that it is weaker, wanting, and for some readers, also unsettling. But this is precisely what happens when a border is crossed, when a new language—or culture, or location—is experienced and absorbed. To immigrate is to observe carefully and copy certain cues. Perhaps total assimilation is not possible, nor even desirable. Each case is different, and each human being who has crossed a border is marked by a unique set of reactions and consequences, resulting in a pattern as distinct as fingerprints.

A language, and by extension a culture, or a nation, that flees its echoes is a culture that is turned inward, in love with itself, or with the idea of itself. We can almost forgive poor Narcissus, who really did believe, foolishly, that the figure in the water, reflected back to him, was someone else. But that someone was just a figment, a shadow. Those who preach to make America great again, or argue for Italians first, are also in love with a shadow. The real America, and the real Italy—the two countries I have come to call home, two extraordinary places full of diversity, cultural richness, and generous souls—don't correspond to the image projected in the water, to a dangerous and solipsistic nostalgia for the past. Those driven to uphold only themselves, to look inward and not outward, have only one outcome. The lines in Ovid are chilling, revealing a state in which all is contorted and convoluted: "Ignorant, he desires himself. The approver is himself approved. / He seeks while being sought. In turns, he kindles and burns" ("se cupit imprudens et qui probat ipse probatur / dumque petit, petitur pariterque accendit et ardet," 425–26). The verbs turn reflexive, eerily echoing one another, and the subject, crouched over himself, implodes and self-destructs. Blind to the truth, Narcissus succumbs to an illusion that deceives him. And Ovid, with his reference to "error," translated here as "illusion," makes quite explicit that his point of view is a mistake: "He knows not what he sees, but what he sees consumes him, / the same illusion tricks and goads his eyes" ("quid uideat nescit, sed quod uidet uritur illo, / atque oculos idem qui decipit incitat error," 430–31). A culture in his position, a nation that adopts this posture, has no choice, like Narcissus himself, but to waste away.

The myth of Echo and Narcissus, which I have only scratched the surface of here, helps me to reflect on the most complicated issue that I have faced thus far in my creative life, which is the act of self-translation. When my first book in Italian was facing the journey into English, I was unwilling, also emotionally incapable, of undertaking that journey myself. The book was translated by another, echoed in another person's English. When I proceeded, tentatively, to translate a short story that I'd written in Italian into English, it felt odd and unnatural, but it was a matter of ten pages, an exercise that ended quickly. I tried to be "faithful" to the original and reproduce a story that was very different, stylistically, from those I had previously written in English. Before the story was published in *The New Yorker* magazine, I had to insist that the phrase "translated by the author" appear at the end of the text. The magazine was initially hesitant, saying that this phrase might appear confusing to readers. I insisted, to honor the nature of the work I had done.

I then faced a new crossroads, and needed to make an important decision. How to bring *Dove mi trovo*, conceived and written in Italian, to English readers? My reluctance to translate myself stemmed partly from the lesson of Narcissus. I feared that turning back to that text, looking at it for a prolonged period in a new language, but nevertheless from my point of view, would be too self-referential, amounting to a hall of mirrors to an infinite and untenable degree. I knew that I would have to re-encounter the same story and reconfigure sentences I'd already written. I wanted to avoid that moment of painful, inevitable recognition when Narcisus exclaims, "I am he!" ("iste ego sum!" 463). At the same time, I would also have to echo myself. It has been said by many that the risk, for the author who self-translates, is to rewrite more than translate, given that there are no rules to obey when the only authority is oneself. What is the meaning of obedience, of faithfulness, when the other does not exist?

When it comes to self-translation, the hierarchy of original and derivation dissolves. To self-translate is to create two originals: twins, far from identical, separately conceived by the same person, who will eventually exist side by side. The relationship between translation and imitation—and, by extension, between Echo and Narcissus—is just as slippery.[3]

---

[3] Most notes that "the precise point at which translation stops and

Let's conclude by returning to our myth. In the end Echo, invisible, deprived of her body, allows Narcissus to utter his final word of adieu. It is with her voice, not his own, that he departs. Though humiliated, she is moved by his tragic end, echoing not only what he says but what he feels: "And yet, though angry, and remembering, / she grieved as she witnessed this, and whenever the wretched boy said 'alas' / she replied, with her resonant voice, 'alas' ("quamuis irata memorque / indoluit, quotiensque puer miserabilis 'eheu!' / dixerat, haec resonis iterabat vocibus 'eheu!' " 494–96). Her behavior is indicative of another one of the translator's necessary traits: empathy. She even accompanies him into the underworld to join those grieving his loss: "When the dryads lamented, Echo accompanied their laments" ("planxerunt Dryades; plangentibus adsonat Echo," 507). Narcissus transforms into a flower, beautiful and alive, yes, but he endures in silence, solitary, lacking compassion or a soul. It is Echo who looks beyond herself, who sings alongside others, who survives him, and whose voice resonates and remains.

Her story and her resilience remind us that translation—which simultaneously repeats, converts, reflects, and restores—is central to the production of literature, not an accessory to it. The richest periods of literary ferment have always been those in which the identities of writers and translators merged, where one activity reinforced and revitalized the other. Classical Rome, the Renaissance, and the fervent translation activity that gained momentum, in Italy, in the 1930s—a period which the critic Emilio Cecchi defined as a "literary revolution"—are just a few examples. The writer who never translates is at a disadvantage in that he or she will be locked, Narcissus-like,

imitation begins is often very hard indeed to discern" (p. 388).

for good or for ill, in an ongoing state of self-reflection. The writer who translates, on the other hand, will both appreciate the limits of any one given language—a crucial awareness, in my opinion—and also take a great leap. The writer who translates will acquire fresh knowledge that springs from less-familiar sources, nourishment which will inevitably lead to broader and deeper literary conversations.[4] Translation will open up entire realms of possibilities, unforeseen pathways that will newly guide and inspire the writer's work, and possibly even transform it. For to translate is to look into a mirror and see someone other than oneself.

ROME, 2019

---

[4] Marius Schneider reminds us, "imitation is knowing. The echo is the paradigmatic form of imitation." (cited in Cirlot, p. xviii)

(5)

An Ode to the Mighty Optative

Notes of a Would-be Translator

φανερὸν δὲ ἐκ τῶν εἰρημένων καὶ ὅτι οὐ τὸ τὰ γενόμενα
λέγειν, τοῦτο ποιητοῦ ἔργον ἐστίν, ἀλλ᾽ οἷα ἂν γένοιτο
καὶ τὰ δυνατὰ κατὰ τὸ εἰκὸς ἢ τὸ ἀναγκαῖον. ὁ γὰρ
ἱστορικὸς καὶ ὁ ποιητὴς οὐ τῷ ἢ ἔμμετρα λέγειν ἢ
ἄμετρα διαφέρουσιν (εἴη γὰρ ἂν τὰ Ἡροδότου εἰς μέτρα
τεθῆναι καὶ οὐδὲν ἧττον ἂν εἴη ἱστορία τις μετὰ μέτρου
ἢ ἄνευ μέτρων)· ἀλλὰ τούτῳ διαφέρει, τῷ τὸν μὲν τὰ
γενόμενα λέγειν, τὸν δὲ οἷα ἂν γένοιτο.
—*POETICS* 1451A-B

ἐπεὶ γάρ ἐστι μιμητὴς ὁ ποιητὴς ὡσπερανεὶ ζωγράφος ἢ
τις ἄλλος εἰκονοποιός, ἀνάγκη μιμεῖσθαι τριῶν ὄντων
τὸν ἀριθμὸν ἕν τι ἀεί, ἢ γὰρ οἷα ἦν ἢ ἔστιν, ἢ οἷά φασιν
καὶ δοκεῖ, ἢ οἷα εἶναι δεῖ.
—*POETICS* 1460B

The citations above, found in two different sections of Aristotle's *Poetics,* were the starting point for a lively discussion at the 2020 Humanities Colloquium at Princeton University. The objective of the colloquium, entitled "Things as They Should Be? A Question for the Humanities," was to consider the philosophical implications of the all-mighty verb *should* across different academic disciplines. Guided by Aristotle's observations, the panelists were asked whether literature could (or should) define expectations, and hence become an instrument for social and political change, and also asked if history also organizes its narratives according to what seems probable or necessary.

My role on the panel was to weigh in as a writer. But, being a translator as well, I was curious to consider alternate English versions of these citations, and felt that I should also put my ancient smattering of Ancient Greek to the test. That the result of my investigations has both clarified and complicated my relationship to what Aristotle is saying about the distinction between poetry and history does not surprise me; this is always the case when we step outside of any given language and venture into another.

In the first citation, Aristotle lays out the difference between the poet and the historian. I began by consulting the English copy of the *Poetics* I happened to have on hand in my study at home, translated by Ingram Bywater in a 1920 edition. One hundred years on, it still reads well, and adheres, so far as I can tell, to Aristotle's syntax in three key points. Bywater's translation contains an introduction by the classicist Gilbert Murray, who writes: "To understand a great foreign book by means of a translation is possible enough where the two languages concerned operate with a common stock of ideas, and belong to the same period of civilization. But between ancient Greece and modern England there yawns immense gulfs of human history." He adds, "Scarcely one in ten of the nouns in the first few pages of the *Poetics* has an exact English equivalent."

With that caveat in mind, here is Bywater's translation of sections 1451a and b:

> From what we have said it will be seen that the poet's function is to describe, not the thing that has happened, but a kind of thing that might happen, i.e. what is possible as being probable or necessary. The distinction between historian and poet is not in the one writing the prose and the other verse—you might put the work of Herodotus into verse, and it would still be a species of history; it consists really in this, that one describes the thing that has been, and the other a kind of thing that might be. (Section 9)

In developing his comparison, Aristotle says something similar twice; the effect resembles an argumentative sandwich, consisting of bread, then filling, then bread. The first slice of bread focuses solely on the poet's function, using a correlative construction signaled by the terms *not* and *but*, which correspond to the negating adverb *ou* and conjunction *alla* (οὐ … ἀλλά) in Greek: hence the poet describes "not the thing that has happened, but a kind of thing that might happen." He then lays down the filling, putting the historian into play, and follows with a second *not*: "the distinction between the historian and the poet is not in the one writing prose and the other writing verse." After referring to Herodotus, he concludes, with a second slice of bread, that the historian relates "the thing that has been," and poet "a kind of thing that might be." This contrast functions not by means of another antithetical *not/but* construction but with *mén* and *dé* (μέν ... δέ) in the Greek, which translates as "on the one hand / on the other." After pitting two ideas against each other, Aristotle ends with a more balanced sentence in which both relative clauses are given equal weight. In that sense, the sandwich analogy no longer functions, for the sequence of not/not/one versus the other suggests a different rhetorical arrangement: that of two slices of bread topped by a filling.

I then turned to a second version, translated by S. H. Butcher, published in 1955. This version, the one I keep in my office at the university, was what I had studied and underlined as a graduate student. Butcher's translation, like Bywater's, also contains the two "not" clauses in the passage, followed by the key concluding sentence—reinforcing what has already been suggested—in which two contrasting ideas coexist:

> It is, moreover, evident from what has been said, that it is not the function of the poet to relate what has happened, but what may happen—what is possible according to the law of probability or necessity. The poet and the historian differ not by writing in verse or in prose. The work of Herodotus might be put into verse, and it would still be a species of history, with meter no less than without it. The true difference is that one relates what has happened, the other what may happen. (*Poetics* IX)

Here, too, we detect the same pattern of not/not/one versus the other. One important difference is that Bywater ends with the verb "be," whereas Butcher chooses "happen." In considering the language of these two versions, I circled in on the terms "might" and "may," auxiliary verbs which appear in each case in the first sentence of the passage, and are repeated in the final clause of the last sentence as well. Bywater opts consistently for "might," Butcher with equal consistency for "may." These verbs are of course closely related in English, one might even say interchangeable, though "might" does double duty as a noun, and is another word for power.

The verb in Aristotle giving rise to the English "might be/ may happen" is γένοιτο/*genoito* (from the infinitive γίγνεσθαι/ *gignesthai*, broadly meaning to be, to be born, to come into being). *Genoito* is a potent verb, and Aristotle employs it in the optative mood, one of the four verbal moods in Ancient Greek, used to express a wish. In dusting off my old Greek grammar, I was reminded that the optative has two main functions: 1) to express wishes for the future, in the spirit of "may," "if only," and "would that," and 2) accompanied by the particle ἄν/ an to indicate that an action might possibly occur. This second instance, known as the potential optative, "corresponds generally to the English potential forms with may, can, might, could, would, etc."[1] This is the optative we find at the end of the first citation by Aristotle.

Latin replaced the optative with the subjunctive, which is the grammatical repository for all things imprecise, uncertain, or otherwise incapable of being pinned down definitively. The subjunctive mood also exists in English, but were most people who speak English asked to explain it, the reply might be rather vague. And yet, any attempt to grapple with Aristotle's passage in English must reckon with the immense gulf between *genoito* as Aristotle intended it and how we in English—deprived of the optative and largely indifferent to the subjunctive—might possibly interpret and engage with it.

As previously mentioned, the title of the colloquium was "Things as They Should Be? A Question for the Humanities":

[1] Goodwin, 281–82.

this title stems not from the aforementioned passage but a later section in the *Poetics*, and it is the second of the citations at the start of this essay. Unlike the first citation, which compares the poet and the historian, this section focuses exclusively on the poet's role.

Here are Bywater's and Butcher's translations, respectively:

The poet being an imitator just like the painter or other maker of likenesses, he must necessarily in all instances represent things in one or other of three aspects, either as they were or are, or as they are said or thought to be or to have been, or as they ought to be.

The poet being an imitator, like a painter or any other artist, must of necessity imitate one of three objects— things as they were or are, things as they are said or thought to be, or things as they ought to be. (Section 25)

The last five words in both translations are identical. Moreover, the "ought" at the end, diluted by a string of other verbs, is presented as an option; indeed, it is one of three, and not the only possible mode of representation. Glancing back at the Greek, I discovered that in this section, Aristotle switches verbs. He does not employ the verb *gignesthai* (which shares the same energy as "happen") but εἶναι/*einai*: a sturdy and stately "to be," as opposed to a wavering but more dynamic "coming into being." Butcher replicates this shift in his use of "happen" in the first citation and "be" in the second, whereas Bywater settles on "be" in both cases. One can only guess which translator Aristotle would have wished on his English readers.

When it comes to literature, wishes are important to keep in mind. One of the first things I learned when I started writing stories was that characters must desire something. And if we unpack the word *desire*, from the Latin *desiderare*, meaning, literally, away from the stars, we learn that every desire implies a distance, an absence, a lack of satisfaction. That longing, that empty space, is where the volcanic potential of the optative *genoito* resides.

This summer a writer friend and I did something that, for decades, we both desired and felt we should do: we read the fourth book of Horace's *Odes* in the original Latin. The first ode we tackled was the tenth. It's called, in David Ferry's translation, "To Ligurinus." In eight lines, Horace addresses a young boy whom he desires. We noted the future tense on four occasions in the Latin. The conceit of the poem is a projection on the poet's part, a theme amplified by the fact that Ligurinus stands in front of a mirror. The poem concludes when Ligurinus, speaking for the first and only time, exclaims, "Alas for what I was / When I was younger than I am, Alas / That then I did not know what I know now; / Alas, that now I know what I did not know."[2] While the triple anaphora of "alas" isn't found (alas!) in the original, Horace's assertion that Ligurinus "will say" this is. But will he? Might Ligurinus's lament not also be the poet's projection?

Ode 10 expresses double desire and double regret: the speaker's unfulfilled desire for Ligurinus, combined with Ligurinus's own remorseful desire for the perspective that once eluded him. One word that struck us was *potens* in the first line, which means powerful, and from which the word *potential* arrives in English. The poem pivots, at the very center, on the participle *mutatus*, meaning changed. No potential can be realized without something becoming something else. The creative process, and also translation, involves a bewildering reaction

2 "dices 'heu' quotiens te in speculo videris alterum, / 'quae mens est hodie, cur eadem non puero fuit, / vel cur his animis incolumes non redeunt genae?'" (5–7)

in which one thing—experience, memory, text—assumes an alternate form. Literature is not normative but speculative, a fact beautifully encapsulated by the mirror in this ode, and further underscored by the final lines in Ferry's translation, which imperfectly reflect one another.

Catapulting forward several centuries: sometimes, when I teach my students how to put a short story together, I have them read a very brief tale by Hemingway called "Cat in the Rain," about a married American couple in an Italian hotel. The conflict is minor and utterly destabilizing. To summarize: the wife notices a cat outside, under a table, but when she tries to retrieve it, it's gone. Frustrated, she sits at the dressing table, in front of a mirror, studying herself, and her longing for the cat triggers desire for other things. First she considers changing her hairstyle, asking: "Don't you think it would be a good idea if I let my hair grow out?" Her wish list accumulates:

> I want to pull my hair back tight and smooth and make a big knot at the back that I can feel ... I want to have a kitty to sit on my lap and purr when I stroke her ... And I want to eat at a table with my own silver and I want candles. And I want it to be spring and I want to brush my hair out in front of a mirror and I want a kitty and I want some new clothes.

Her husband tells her to shut up and read a book. His response, at the end of her list of desires, is to behave as if she were merely complaining.

Just as hope is built into the very grammar of Ancient Greek, so is it an essential element of this dark story. Hemingway never explicitly says this; the emotional truth remains contrary to the facts, rooted in the realm of "might." The story, light-years from Aristotle, nevertheless conveys the force of *genoito*—things as they might be. In other words, a year from now, the couple in the hotel might no longer be together. Like Horace, Hemingway plays with a mirror, with repetition, and with time, projecting forward to a moment and place the story's structure can't attain.

Things are seldom as they should be, which is why we spend so much time and energy wishing they could be different. The writer Mavis Gallant talks about the impulse to write as stemming from "the shock of change," which she describes as follows: "Probably, it means a jolt that unbolts the door between perception and imagination and leaves it ajar for life, or that fuses memory and language and waking dreams. Some writers may just simply come into the world with overlapping visions of things seen and things as they might be seen." (p. xv)

While the shock of change is often a catalyst for art, art is not—should not—be an instrument for change of any kind. Once art weds itself to a social or political purpose it is bled of its true purpose, which is not to change the world but to explore the phenomenon and the consequences of change itself. While history archives and evaluates change, art, as it's been said by Shakespeare and others, holds up a mirror, the same one Horace inserted into his ode and Hemingway placed in his story. Aristotle, too, in the brief citation I studied, nearly mirrors his own words in the course of making his point. In observing and imitating life, art, like Aristotle, shrewdly oscillates between alternate versions of who and what and why we are.

The word for the optative in Greek comes from the verb εὔχεσθαι/*euchesthai* : to pray, to beseech, to long for. If literature were its own language—and I believe that it is—its principal mood would be the optative. For literature, like the optative, projects beyond the here and now, and sometimes wishes, fiercely, that things might have played out differently.

Were I to fulfill a wish—were I to resurrect the Ancient Greek I learned long ago, and translate the first passage by Aristotle—I would emphasize "might" as opposed to "may." "May" is not a wrong choice, just as "might" is not necessarily the right one. Translation is about choosing, at times wisely, at times reluctantly, always with lingering misgivings (and here it is opportune to recall that in Latin, *optare* means both to choose and to wish). Translation generates innumerable "mights" and relatively few "shoulds," causing meaning to keep leaning, like a boat on swelling seas, from one side to another. In fact, the "should" that was the premise of our colloquium is in direct contradiction to the imagination and to creativity, which are governed by sibylline, erratic forces, not necessarily plausible ones.

Through translation, the two meanings of the word *might* in English, as verb and noun, as power and possibility, now strike me as revelatory and, yes, poetic, as does the Horace's *potens*, which is the term for "powerful" and comes from *posse*, the verb that signifies "to be able"—that is, to have the means, strength, capacity, permission, power, and freedom—to do something. But that freedom is never a given. The writer has always depended on the means, strength, capacity, permission, power, and above all, the freedom to fill the page, with either a single word or as many as will fit in the space, without "should" lurking in the corner. The mightiness of literature—its infinite potential—lies there.

ROME, 2020

(6)

Where I Find Myself

On Self-Translation

Having written my novel *Dove mi trovo* in Italian, I was the first to doubt that it could transform into English. Naturally it could be translated; any text can, with greater or lesser degrees of success. I was not apprehensive when translators began turning the novel into other languages—into Spanish or German or Dutch, for example. Rather, the prospect gratified me. But when it came to replicating this particular book, conceived and written in Italian, into the language that I knew best—the language I had emphatically stepped away from in order for it to be born in the first place—I was of two minds.

As I was writing *Dove mi trovo*, the thought of it being anything other than an Italian text felt irrelevant. While writing, one must keep one's eyes on the road, straight ahead, and not contemplate or anticipate driving down another. The dangers, for the writer as for the driver, are obvious.

And yet, even as I was writing, I felt shadowed by two questions: 1) when would the text be turned into English, and

2) who would translate it? These questions rose from the fact that I am also, and was for many years exclusively, a writer in English. And so, if I choose to write in Italian, the English version immediately rears its head, like a bulb that sprouts too early in mid-winter. Everything I write in Italian is born with the simultaneous potential—or perhaps destiny is the better word here—of existing in English. Another image, perhaps jarring, comes to mind: that of the burial plot of a surviving spouse, demarcated and waiting.

The responsibility of translation is as grave and precarious as that of a surgeon who is trained to transplant organs, or to redirect the blood flow to our hearts, and I wavered at length over the question of who would perform the surgery. I thought back to other authors who had migrated into different languages. Had they translated their own work? And if so, where did translation taper off, and the act of rewriting take over? I was wary of betraying myself. Beckett had notably altered his French when translating himself into English. Brodsky, too, took great liberties when translating his Russian poetry into English. Juan Rodolfo Wilcock, an Argentine whose major works were composed in Italian, had been more "faithful" when rendering his texts into Spanish. Another Argentine, Borges, who had grown up bilingual in Spanish and English, translated numerous works into Spanish, but left the English translation of his own work to others. Leonora Carrington, whose first language was English, had also left to someone else the messy business of translating many of her French and Spanish stories, as had the Italian writer Antonio Tabucchi in the case of *Requiem*, the great novel he wrote in Portuguese.

When an author migrates into another language, the subsequent crossing into the former language might be regarded, by some, as a crossing back, an act of return, a coming home.

This idea is false, and it was also not my objective. Even before I decided to translate *Dove mi trovo* myself, I knew that the idea of "coming home" was no longer an option. I had gone too deep into Italian, and so English no longer represented the reassuring, essential act of coming up for air. My center of gravity had shifted; or at least, it had begun to shift back and forth.

* * *

I began writing *Dove mi trovo* in the spring of 2015. I had been living in Italy for three years, but had already made the anguished decision to return to the United States. As with most projects, in the beginning, I had no sense that the words I was scribbling in a notebook would develop into a book. When I left Rome in August of that year, I took the notebook with me. It languished in my study in Brooklyn, though in retrospect "hibernated" is the apt term, for when I returned to Rome that winter, I found myself turning back to the notebook, which had traveled with me, and adding new scenes. The following year I moved to Princeton, New Jersey. But every two months or so I flew to Rome, either for short stays or for the summer, always with the notebook in my carry-on suitcase, and by 2017, once the notebook was full, I began to type out the contents.

In 2018, on sabbatical, I was able to move back to Rome for an entire year for the book's publication. When asked about the English version, I said that it was still too soon to think about it. In order to undertake a translation, or even to evaluate a translation someone else has done, one must understand the particulars of the book in question, just as the surgeon, ideally, needs to study her patient's organism before entering the operating room. I knew that I needed time—a great deal of it—to pass. I needed to gain distance from the novel, answer questions about it, hear responses from my Italian readers. For, though I'd already written the book, I felt the way my own immigrant parents perhaps felt as they were raising me: the author of an inherently foreign creature, both recognizable and unrecognizable, born from my flesh and blood.

Regarding the eventual English translation, two camps quickly formed. Members of the first camp were those who urged me to translate the book myself. Their opponents urged me, with equal vehemence, to steer clear of the operation. To return to my analogy of the surgeon, I sometimes said, to members of the first camp, What surgeon, in need of an operation, would take the scalpel to herself? Wouldn't she entrust the procedure to another pair of hands?

Following the advice of Gioia Guerzoni, an Italian translator friend who belonged to the second camp, I sought out the translator Frederika Randall, who worked out of Italian into English. Frederika was an American based in Rome for decades, not far from where I lived: the very part of the city where my book, loosely speaking (though I never specify this), is set. When she said she was willing to translate the first dozen or so pages, so that we could both get a feel for how her translation would sound, I was relieved. I was convinced that she was the ideal person to translate my novel, not only because she was an extremely skilled translator, but because she knew the setting and atmosphere of the book far better than I did.

I thought that perhaps, once she'd finished the translation, I could weigh in on one or two matters, and that my role would be respectfully collaborative. Grandmotherly, which was how I felt when Mira Nair had turned one of my other novels into a film. Perhaps this time I would be a slightly more involved grandmother than I had been to Ann Goldstein's translation of *In Other Words* (produced at a time when I was wary of any reconnection with English, and did not relish at all the role of being a grandmother). Deep down, however, I was convinced that when I saw the English version, it would reveal, brusquely and definitively, the book's failure to function in English, not due to any fault of Frederika, but because the book itself, inherently flawed, would refuse to comply, like a potato or an apple that, decayed within, must be set aside once it is cut open and examined, and cannot lend itself to any other dish.

Instead, when I read the pages she prepared for me, I found that the book was intact, that the sentences made sense, and that the Italian had enough sap to sustain another text in another language. At this point a surprising thing happened. I switched camps and felt the urge to take over, just as, watching my daughter turn somersaults underwater this past summer, I, too, was inspired to learn how. Of course, that discombobulating act of flipping over, the idea of which had always terrified me until the day I finally figured out, thanks to my daughter, how to execute the maneuver, was exactly what my own book had to do. Frederika, who had lived astride English and Italian for so very long, was bipartisan to the core. She had understood, initially, why I'd been reluctant to translate the book myself, and when I told her I was having a change of heart, she wasn't surprised. Like my daughter, she encouraged me. As is often the case when crossing a new threshold, it had taken her example, just like my daughter's, to show me that it could be done.

I was still in Rome—a place where I feel no inspiration to work out of Italian into English—when I came to my decision. When living and writing in Rome, I have an Italian center of gravity. I needed to move back to Princeton, where I am surrounded by English, where I miss Rome. Italian translation, for me, has always been a way to maintain contact with the language I love when I am far away from it. To translate is to alter one's linguistic coordinates, to grab on to what has slipped away, to cope with exile.

* * *

I began translating in 2019, at the start of the fall semester. I didn't look at Frederika's sample pages; in fact, I hid them away. The book consists of forty-six relatively brief chapters. I aimed to tackle one at each sitting, two or three sittings per week. I approached the text and it greeted me like certain neighbors— if not warmly, politely enough. As I felt my way back into the book, and pressed through it, it yielded discreetly. There were roadblocks now and then, and I stopped to ponder them, or I stepped over them, determined, before stopping to think too much about what I was doing, to reach the end.

One obvious roadblock was the title itself. The literal translation, which means "where I find myself," sounded belabored to me. The book had no English title until, at the end of October, with a few chapters still left to translate, I stepped on a plane to go to Rome. Not long after takeoff, "whereabouts" popped into my brain: a word as inherently English, and as fundamentally untranslatable, as the expression *dove mi trovo* is in Italian. Somewhere in the air, over the waters that separate my English and Italian lives, the original title recognized itself—dare I say found itself—in another language.

Once I finished the first draft, I circulated it to a small group of readers who did not read Italian, who knew me well, and only, as a writer in English. Then I waited, anxiously, even though the book had already been born over a year before, and was already living, not only in Italian but, as previously mentioned, in other languages as well. It was only after these readers told me the book had spoken to them that I believed that the foolhardy operation I had performed on myself had not been in vain.

As *Dove mi trovo* was turning into *Whereabouts*, I naturally had to keep referring back to the original book I'd written. I began to notice a few repetitions in the Italian I wished I'd caught. Certain adjectives I was relying on too heavily. A few inconsistencies. I had miscounted the number of people at a dinner party, for example. I began to mark the Italian book with adhesive arrows, and then to keep a list to send to my Italian editors at Guanda, so that certain changes could be made in subsequent editions of the book. In other words, the second version of the book was now generating a third: a revised Italian text that was stemming from my self-translation. When translating oneself, each and every flaw or weakness in the former text becomes immediately and painfully apparent. Keeping to my medical metaphors, I would say that self-translation is like one of those radioactive dyes that enable doctors to look through our skin to locate damage in the cartilage, unfortunate blockages, and other states of imperfection.

As discomfiting as this process of revelation was, I felt a parallel gratitude for the very ability to isolate these problems, to be aware of them and to find new solutions. The brutal act of self-translation frees oneself, once and for all, from the false myth of the definitive text. It was only by self-translating that I finally understood what Paul Valéry meant when he said that a work of art was never finished, only abandoned. The publication of any book is an arbitrary act; there is no ideal phase of gestation, nor of birth, as is the case for living creatures. A book is done when it seems done, when it feels done, when the author is sick of it, or is eager to publish it, or when the editor wrests it away. All of my books, in retrospect, feel premature. The act of self-translation enables the author to restore a previously published work to its most vital and dynamic state—that of a work-in-progress—and to repair and recalibrate as needed.

Some people insist that there is no such thing as self-translation, and that it necessarily becomes an act of rewriting or emphatically editing—read: improving—the first go-around. This temptation attracts some and repels others. I personally was not interested in altering my Italian book in order to arrive at a more supple, elegant, and mature version of it in English. My aim was to respect and reproduce the novel I had originally conceived, but not so blindly as to reproduce and perpetuate certain infelicities.

As *Whereabouts* moved through copyediting to typeset pages, with different editors and proofreaders weighing in, so did the changes to *Dove mi trovo* continue to accumulate—I repeat, all relatively minor, but nevertheless significant to me. The two texts began to move forward in tandem, each on its own terms. When the paperback of *Dove mi trovo* eventually comes out in Italian—at the time of writing, it hasn't yet—I will consider it the definitive version, at least for now, given that I have come to think of any "definitive text" largely the same way that I think of a mother tongue, at least in my case: an inherently debatable, perpetually relative concept.

* * *

The first day I sat down with the page proofs of *Whereabouts*, during the autumn of the coronavirus pandemic, I went to Princeton's Firestone Library, booking a seat and taking my place at a round white marble table. I was masked and many feet away from the other three people allowed in a room that could easily hold one hundred. I realized that day, when pausing to

question something in the English text, that I had left my bat-
tered copy of *Dove mi trovo* at home. The translator side of me,
focused on bringing the book into English, was already sub-
consciously distancing and disassociating from the Italian. Of
course, it is always strange, and also crucial, at the last phase
of looking at a translation, to all but disregard the text in the
original language. The latter cannot be hovering, as I did when
my children first went off to school, somewhere in the building, alert to cries of protest. A true separation, as false as that
is, must occur. In the final stages of reviewing a translation,
either of one's own work or someone else's, one achieves a level
of concentration that is akin to focusing purely on the quality
and sensations of the water when one is swimming in the sea,
as opposed to admiring elements that float through it or collect
on the seabed. When one is so focused on language, a selective
blindness sets in, and along with it, a form of X-ray vision.

Reading over the page proofs of *Whereabouts* in English, I
began reflecting in my diary, in Italian, on the process of having translated it. In fact, the text you are now reading, which I've
written in English, is a product of notes taken in Italian. In
some sense, this is the first piece of writing that I have conceived
bilingually, and so the subject, self-translation, feels especially
appropriate. Here, in translation, are some of the notes I took:

1. The profoundly destabilizing thing about self-translation
   is that the book threatens to unravel, to hurtle toward
   potential annihilation. It seems to annihilate itself.
   Or am I annihilating it? No text should sustain that
   level of scrutiny; at a certain point, it cedes. It's the reading and the scrutinizing, the insistent inquiry implicit
   in the act of writing and translating, that inevitably
   jostle the text.

2. This task is not for the faint of heart. It forces you to doubt the validity of every word on the page. It casts your book—already published, between covers, sold on shelves in stores—into a revised state of profound uncertainty. It is an operation that feels doomed from the start, even contrary to nature, like the experiments of Victor Frankenstein.

3. Self-translation is a bewildering, paradoxical going backward and moving forward at once. There is ongoing tension between the impulse to plow ahead, undermined by a strange gravitational force that holds you back. One feels silenced in the very act of speaking. Those two dizzying tercets from Dante come to mind, with their language of doubling and their contorted logic: "Qual è colui che suo dannaggio sogna, / che sognando desidera sognare, / sì che quel ch'è, come non fosse, agogna, // tale me fec'io, non possendo parlare, / che disïava scusarmi, e scusava / me tuttavia, e nol mi credea fare" (*Inferno* XXX, lines 136–41). ("Like one asleep who dreams himself in trouble / and in his dream he wishes he were dreaming, / longing for that which is, as if it were not, // just so I found myself: unable to speak, / longing to beg for pardon and already / begging for pardon, not knowing that I did."[1]

4. Reading the English, every sentence that felt off, that had gone astray in the translation, always led me back to a misreading of myself in Italian.

---

[1] Dante Alighieri, *The Divine Comedy*, vol. 1: *Inferno*, trans. Mark Musa, p. 347.

5. *Whereabouts* will emerge on its own, without the Italian text on the facing page, as was the case with *In Other Words*. But if anything, the absence of the Italian reinforces, for me, the bond between these two versions, one of which I wrote, and one of which I translated. These two versions have entered into a tennis match. But in fact, it's the ball that represents both texts, volleyed from one side of the net over the other and back again.

6. Self-translation means prolonging your relationship to the book you've written. Time expands and the sun still shines when you expect things to go dark. This disorienting surplus of daylight feels unnatural, but it also feels advantageous, magical.

7. Self-translation affords a second act for a book, but in my opinion, this second act pertains less to the translated version than to the original, which is now readjusted and realigned thanks to the process of being dismantled and reassembled.

8. What I altered in Italian was what, in hindsight, still felt superfluous to my view. The stringent quality of English forced the Italian text, at times, to tighten its belt as well.

9. I suppose the exhilarating aspect of translating myself was being constantly reminded, as I changed the words from one language to another, that I myself had changed so profoundly, and that I was capable of such change. I realized that my relationship to

the English language, thanks to my linguistic graft, had also been irrevocably altered.

10. *Whereabouts* will never be an autonomous text in my mind, nor will the paperback of *Dove mi trovo*, which is now indebted to the process of first translating and then revising *Whereabouts*. They share the same vital organs. They are conjoined twins, though, on the surface, they bear no resemblance to one another. They have nourished and been nourished by the other. Once the translation was in progress, I almost felt like a passive bystander as they began sharing and exchanging elements between themselves.

11. I believe I began writing in Italian to obviate the need to have an Italian translator. As grateful as I am to those who have rendered my English books into Italian in the past, something was driving me, in Italian, to speak for myself. I have now assumed the role I had set out to eliminate, only in the inverse. Becoming my own translator in English has only lodged me further inside the Italian language.

12. In some sense the book remains Italian in my head in spite of its metamorphosis into English. The adjustments I made in English were always in service to the original text.

* * *

In reviewing the proofs of *Whereabouts*, I noticed a sentence I'd skipped entirely in the English. It has to do with the word *portagioie,* which, in the Italian version, the protagonist considers the most beautiful word in the Italian language. But the sentence only carries its full weight in Italian. The English equivalent of *portagioie*, "jewelry box," doesn't contain the poetry of *portagioie,* given that joys and jewels are not the same thing in English. I inserted the sentence into the translation, but had to alter it. This is probably the most significantly reworked bit of the book, and I added a footnote for clarification. I had hoped to avoid footnotes, but in this case, the "I" in Italian and the "I" in English had no common ground.

The penultimate chapter of the novel is called "*Da nessuna parte.*" I translated it as "Nowhere" in English, which breaks the play of prepositions in the English titles. An Italian reader pointed this out, suggesting I translate it more literally as "In no place." I considered making the change, but in the end my English ear prevailed, and I opted for an adverb which, to my satisfaction, contains the "where" of the title I'd come up with.

There was one instance of grossly mistranslating myself. It was a crucial line, and I only caught the error in the final pass. As I was reading the English proofs aloud for the last time, without referring back to the Italian, I knew the sentence was wrong, and that I had completely, unintentionally mangled the meaning of my own words.

It also took several readings to correct an auxiliary verb in English that the Italian side of my brain, in the act of translating, had rendered sloppily. In English one *takes steps,* but in Italian one *makes* them. Given that I read and write in both languages, my brain has developed blind spots. It was only by looking again and again at the English that I saved a character in *Whereabouts* from "making steps." Having said this, in English, it is possible to make missteps.

In the end, the hardest thing about translating *Whereabouts* were the lines written not by me but by two other writers: Italo Svevo—whom I cite in the epigraph—and Corrado Alvaro, whom I cite in the body of the text. Their words, not mine, are the ones I feel ultimately responsible for, and have wrestled with most. These are the lines I will continue to fret over even when the book goes to press. The desire to translate—to press up as closely as possible to the words of another, to cross the threshold of one's consciousness—is keener when the other remains inexorably, incontrovertibly out of reach.

* * *

I believe it was important to have gained experience translating other authors out of Italian before confronting *Dove mi trovo*. The upsetting experience of trying to translate myself early on in the process of writing in Italian, which I briefly touched upon in *In Other Words*, had a lot to do with the fact that I had yet to translate anyone else out of Italian. All my energy back then was devoted to sinking deeper into the new language and avoiding English as much as possible. I had to establish myself as a translator of others before I could achieve the illusion of being another myself.

As someone who dislikes looking back at her work, and prefers not to reread it if at all possible, I was not an ideal candidate to translate *Dove mi trovo*, given that translation is the most intense form of reading and rereading there is. I have never reread one of my books as many times as *Dove mi trovo*. The experience would have been deadening had it been one of my English books. But working with Italian, even a book that I have myself composed slips surprisingly easily in and out of my hands. This is because the language resides both within me and beyond my grasp. The author who wrote *Dove mi trovo* both is and is not the author who translated them. This split consciousness is, if nothing else, a bracing experience.

For years I have trained myself, when asked to read aloud from my work, to approach it as if it had been written by someone else. Perhaps my impulse to separate radically from my former work, book after book, was already conditioning me to recognize the separate writers who have always dwelled inside me. We write books in a fixed moment in time, in a specific phase of our consciousness and development. That is why reading words written years ago feels alienating. You are no longer the person whose existence depended on the production of those words. But alienation, for better or for worse, establishes distance, and grants perspective, two things that are particularly crucial to the act of self-translation.

Self-translation led to a deep awareness of the book I'd written, and therefore, to one of my past selves. As I've said, once I write my other books, I tend to walk away as quickly as possible, whereas I now have a certain residual affection for *Dove mi trovo*, just as I do for its English counterpart—an affection born from the intimacy that can only be achieved by the collaborative act of translating as opposed to the solitary act of writing.

I also feel, toward *Dove mi trovo*, a level of acceptance that I have not felt for the other books. The others still haunt me with choices I might have made, ideas I ought to have developed, passages that should have been further revised. In translating *Dove mi trovo*, in writing it a second time in a second language and allowing it to be born, largely intact, a second time, I feel closer to it, doubly tied to it, whereas the other books represent a series of relationships, passionate and life-altering at the time, that have now cooled to embers, never having strayed beyond the point of no return.

My copy of *Dove mi trovo* in Italian is a now dog-eared volume, underlined and marked with Post-its indicating the various corrections and clarifications to be made. It has transformed from a published text to something resembling a set of bound galleys. I would never have thought to make those changes had I not translated the book out of the language in which I conceived and created it. Only I was capable of accessing and altering both texts from the inside. Now that the book is about to be printed in English, it has traded places with the finished Italian copy, which has lost its published patina, at least from the author's point of view, and resumed the identity of a work still in its final stages of becoming a published text. As I write this, *Whereabouts* is being sewn up for publication, but *Dove mi trovo* needs to be opened up again for a few discreet procedures. That original book, which now feels incomplete to me, stands in line behind its English-language counterpart. Like an image viewed in the mirror, it has turned into the simulacrum, and both is and is not the starting point for what rationally and irrationally followed.

PRINCETON, 2020

(7)

Substitution

Afterword to Trust *by Domenico Starnone*

To write, first and foremost, is to choose the words to tell a story, whereas to translate is to evaluate, acutely, each word an author chooses. Repetitions in particular rise instantly to the surface, and they give the translator particular pause when there is more than one way to translate a particular word. On the one hand, why not repeat a word the author has deliberately repeated? On the other hand, was the repetition deliberate? Regardless of the author's intentions, the translator's other ear, in the other language, opens the floodgates to other solutions.

The Italian word that caught my ear above all others in this novel was *invece*. It appears three times in the volcanic first paragraph, and occurs a total of sixty-four times from beginning to end. *Invece*, which pops up constantly in Italian conversation, was a familiar word to me. It means "instead" and serves as an umbrella for words like "rather," "on the contrary," "however," "meanwhile," and "in fact." A compound of the preposition *in* and the noun *vece*—the latter means "place" or "stead"—it derives from the Latin *invicem*, which in turn is a compound of *in* and the noun *vicis*, declined as *vice* in the ablative case. When, after completing a first draft of my translation of *Trust*, I looked up *vicis* in a few Latin dictionaries, in both Italian and English, I found the following definitions: *change, exchange, interchange, alternation, succession, requital, recompense, retaliation, repayment, place, room, post, office, plight, lot, time, occasion, opportunity, event,* and, in the plural, *danger or risk.*

But let's move forward on the linguistic timeline and back to the Italian term, *invece,* of which Starnone seems either consciously or unwittingly fond. Functioning as an adverb in Italian, it is a word that links one concept to another, that pits one notion against another, that establishes a relationship between different ideas. *Invece* invites one thing to substitute for another, and its robust Latin root gives rise in English to "vice versa" (literally, "the order being changed"), the prefix *vice* (as in the vice president who must stand in for the president if need be), and the word *vicissitude,* which means a passing from one state of affairs to the next. Based on my investigation of *invece* across three languages, I now believe that this everyday Italian adverb is the metaphorical underpinning of Starnone's novel. For if *Ties* is an act of containment and *Trick* an interplay of juxtaposition, *Trust* probes and prioritizes substitution: an operation that not only permeates the novel's arc but describes the process of my bringing it into English. In other words, I believe that *invece,* a trigger for substitution, is a metaphor for translation itself.

Invece insists that circumstances are always changing—that, without a variation to the norm, there is no jagged line of plot, only the flat fact of situation. Starnone's penchant for the term reminds us that, essentially, there is no plot of any book, in any language, in which the notion of *invece* is not complicating matters and thus propelling the action forward. It points all the way back to *polytropos*, the epithet Homer uses to describe Odysseus at the start of his epic poem: he is the man of "many twists and turns." To repeat, it is only when one reality or experience or inclination is thrown into question by another that a story gets going.

Fittingly, there is a teeter-totter element running through *Trust*, though a more high-adrenaline diversion, roller coasters, now comes to mind (*nota bene:* roller coasters are also referred to as "twisters" in English). Starnone often pauses at the precise moment in which the roller coaster, creeping upward on its trajectory, briefly pauses before hurtling back down. He emphasizes this moment of drastic transition with phrases like *proprio mentre* or *proprio quando*—I translate them as " just as" or "just when" in Italian. Each time, it signals a plunge, a lurch, a swoop, a turning upside-down. The laws of Starnone's fictional universe, which correspond to the universe in general, remind us that everything in life is always on the brink of altering, vanishing, or turning on its head. At times these changes (or rather, vicissitudes) are miraculous and moving. At other times, they are traumatic and terrifying. In Starnone's pages, they are always both, and what one appreciates by reading him, and especially by translating him, is just how skilled he is when it comes to crafting and calibrating fictional time: how nimbly he curves and tilts it, bends and weaves it, slows it down, speeds it up, enables it to climb and fall. He builds to breathtaking panoramas and, the next instant, induces heart-dropping anxiety, primal screams, and hysterical laughter. Something tells me that Starnone has a hell of a good time laying down these tracks.

Places change, our preference and predilections change, people and politics change. Like many of Starnone's novels, this one toggles between past and present, between Naples and Rome, between starting out in life and taking stock in old age. But the most significant reversal is that of roles, between teacher and student. The student-teacher dynamic is familiar to most of us, given that most of us have been students at one time or another. It just so happens that Starnone (and his present translator) have also been on the teaching side of this equation. It also just so happens that this novel is very much about the education system: what it means to teach and to be taught, and why teachers must always learn to teach better. But what is a teacher, other than a former student whose role has been replaced by another? Where does the student taper off and the teacher take over? And what happens when a student goes on to learn more than her teacher, and ends up teaching him a thing or two? This novel recounts a love affair between a male teacher and a former female student: nothing new there, other than the fact that, in a post-#MeToo era, our reading of (and tolerance for) such relationships may have changed. The passage from student to teacher involves a succession, just as the passage from childhood to adulthood, from lover to spouse, from parent to grandparent. No role is ever a fixed role, and this novel traces how one's station in life always wavers as characters shift from obscurity to success, from trying economic circumstances to more comfortable ones. And it traces the vagaries of the human heart, of desire. So much drama is born from the impulse to substitute the person we think we love with another, especially when children are involved.

There is an exchange of words at the heart of this book, words that are never revealed to the reader. This secret exchange of information determines the destinies of two characters—of Pietro, the male protagonist, above all. What is said between the characters (but left unsaid on the page) threatens to overthrow everything—and to introduce chaos, which is always lapping at the shores of everyday mortal reality in Starnone's works. The potential earthquake in *Trust*, at least from Pietro's point of view, regards what a former lover might say about him. Maintaining order (not to mention ensuring that the conventional "plot" of Pietro's life unfolds without incident) depends on not saying things. We can trace a constellation from Dante to Manzoni to Hemingway to Starnone that sheds light on how writers use language to talk about silence and the importance of withholding speech. But the exchange embedded under the iceberg of *Trust* also carries the threat of retribution, and is a source of peril.

What an intelligent, articulate woman might say has always been considered dangerous. In Ovid's *Metamorphoses*—a work I happen to be translating as I write these words about Starnone—they have their tongues cut out, or are reduced to echoes, or turn into trees who merely rustle their leaves in acknowledgment, or into animals who moo instead of utter sentences. In Ovid, these states of transformation (or mutation) involve a partial or full muting of the female voice, and even mutilation. They may be read both as liberation from—and the consequences of—patriarchal power and predatory behaviors. If we break down the moment of metamorphosis in almost any episode in Ovid, the effect is one of substitution: of body parts being replaced by other anatomical features, one by one. That is to say, hooves appear instead of feet, or branches instead of arms.[1] This systematic substitution is what allows, in Ovid, for

---

[1] Inspired by my study of *invece* in *Trust*, I am now tracking recurrences of the term *vicis* in the *Metamorphoses*. I'll share, here, two instances in book 4: In line 40 (the myth of the Minyeides), "perque uices," meaning "by turns," and line 218 (the myth of Clytie and Leucothoe), "noxque uicem peragit," meaning "and night takes a turn." The first instance refers to the alternating trajectory storytelling; the second to the turning of time.

a complete and comprehensive change of form. Not always, but often, Ovid walks us through the metamorphosis step by step, slowing things down so that we understand exactly how dynamic and dramatic the process is.

Translation, too, is a dynamic and dramatic transformation. Word for word, sentence for sentence, page for page, until a text conceived and written and read in one language comes to be reconceived, rewritten, and read in another. The translator labors to find alternative solutions, not to cancel out the original, but to counter it with another version. My version of this book was produced to stand in the place of the Italian, so that readers in English might have a relationship with it. It is now an English book instead of—*invece di*—an Italian one.

Even within a single language, one word can so very often substitute another. As I said earlier, it is the writer's job, and subsequently the translator's, to choose among them. While the writer typically has one go, translation extends this game and complicates it significantly. Given that there are so often multiple terms to say the same thing, we are all playing the substitution game in the way we think, speak, write, and otherwise express ourselves. The dictionary reminds us that there are more synonyms than antonyms. Not all words have an opposite, but the vast majority have stand-ins to augment our understanding, interpretation, and use of them.

Take the Italian word *anzi*, for example, which also appears quite frequently in this novel. It can function as a preposition or an adverb, and it can mean "actually," "on the contrary," "rather," "indeed," and "in fact." In fact, *anzi* can substitute for *invece*, given that if one appends the conjunction *che* to *anzi*, ("instead of," "rather than") it essentially means the same thing as *invece di*. Like *invece*, *anzi* is a syntactical fly in the ointment that draws our attention to a hidden scenario, a hiccup, a twist of fate or mood or point of view. Deriving from the Latin preposition and prefix *ante-*, it posits—in English, too—that time has passed, that things are no longer as they previously were, that a different moment preceded this one; indeed, that you are reading this sentence in this moment as opposed to another.

In this novel there are two terms used for the deepest and potentially most destabilizing emotion we human beings can experience. One is the verb *amare*, which means "to love," and gives us the noun *love* (*amore*), which is the novel's first word, and that reinforces the link between *Trust* and Ovid, author of not only the *Ars amatoria* (*The Art of Love*) but also, of course, the changing love stories running through the *Metamorphoses*. For the question that drives this book forward is one anyone who has ever loved has likely reckoned with: What happens when love alters; when it cools, melts, or softens; when it makes room for another? Shakespeare's Sonnet 116 tells us that "Love is not love / Which alters when it alteration finds"; and yet, all the words pertaining to altering and bending in Shakespeare's poem give us pause, and they pave the way for Starnone's steadfast attention to amatory impediments. But in addition to *amare*, Starnone pulls the expression *voler bene* into the mix. There is no satisfying English solution for this Italian phrase. Literally, it means to want good things for someone, to wish someone well. But in Italian what it actually means is to feel affection for someone, and thus to love someone, both in a romantic and nonromantic sense. *Amare* and *voler bene* are to some degree interchangeable, and yet they are very distinct. They can have different connotations in different regions of Italy, and can suggest one type of love as opposed to another.

An interesting distinction: one can *amare* many things, but one can only *voler bene* another person or personified object. *Amare* derives from Latin, as does *voler bene*. Catullus combines these sentiments in poem 72, which begins by comparing his love for Lesbia to a father's fondness for his children. That is to say, the poet's love for her has surpassed the conventional emotional tie between lovers, which is subject to change. The end of the poem reads: "quod amantem iniuria talis / cogit amare magis, sed bene velle minus." (My English translation would be: "because such harm / drives the lover to love more, but like less," though Francis Warre Cornish's prose translation reads: "Because such an injury as this drives a lover to be more of a lover, but less of a friend."[2]) The last line, which has been described as "perfectly balanced,"[3] is poised on the conjunction *sed*, meaning but, which, like *invece*, places two ideas in conversation, the latter modifying the former. In Italian translations, "bene velle" turns into *voler bene*, and indicates friendship as opposed to romantic love or, if you will, liking as opposed to loving.[4]

Amare and *voler bene* command our attention in *Trust* from the very beginning; these terms are what we get to know first, and they, along with change, are the real protagonists of Starnone's novel. Think of them as good witch and bad witch; I won't say which is which. The degree to which they overlap and challenge each other, the way they correspond with and compete with and cancel one another—much like *invece* and

---

[2] "The Poems of Gaius Valerius Catullus," translated by F. W. Cornish, (Cambridge, Massachusetts: Harvard University Press, 1988).

[3] *Catullus: The Shorter Poems*, edited with introduction, translation, and commentary by John Godwin (Warminster, England: Aris & Phillips Ltd, 1999).

[4] *Velle*, an infinitive meaning "to wish or want" in Latin, is just one letter away from Vella, the protagonist's last name. *Vello*, meanwhile, is another Latin verb that means "I pluck/I pull/I destroy."

anzi—proves that language—or rather, the combination of language and human usage—is impossible to comprehend at face value. We must enter, instead, into a more profound relationship with words—we must descend with them to a deeper level, uncovering layers of alternatives in a hidden and hermetic realm. The only way to even begin to understand language is to love it so much that we allow it to confound us and to torment us to the extent that it threatens to swallow us whole.

Across the three books, it's been a challenge to substitute Starnone's crisp single-word titles in Italian with a satisfying word in English. Here is the first instance when the original title, *Confidenza*, might have simply been substituted with the English cognate, "Confidence." And yet I chose differently. Like *confidenza*, the word *confidence* has multiple meanings in English: intimacy, secrecy, and assurance. Starnone's title is bolstered, thematically, by all three meanings. But in Italian *confidenza* points more to the idea of a secret exchange, as opposed to the English sense of assurance or certitude. My choice of "trust" is linked to the intimate relationship recounted in this novel, and the precarious psychological game that ensues. Interestingly, it is the Latin *confidentia* that is closer to the English connotations of boldness, audacity, and impudence. I justify my choice in the end because the first definition of the verb *confido* in my Latin dictionary is, in fact, "to trust."[5] Though, come to think of it, I might have called this novel *Twist* or *Turn* instead.

This is the third of Starnone's novels I have translated in a span of six years, and it completes a certain cycle. It is not the final installment of a trilogy, but certainly the third side of a triangle. All three books feature diverse first-person narrators,

---

[5] Lewis, Charlton T. *An Elementary Latin Dictionary: With Brief Helps for Latin Readers* (Oxford: Oxford University Press, 1985).

tense marriages, fraught relationships between parent and child. Running themes include a quest for liberty, the collision of past and present, building a career, fear, aging, anger, mediocrity, talent, and competition. Read in a row, one seems to emerge from the next. But for those who have read the rest of Starnone's considerable body of work, this final installment is in conversation with those that precede it; and for those reading between the lines, there is not only a great deal of intertextuality with other authors but a subtle "intratextuality" with previous works—Starnone standing in for other Starnones, for prior Starnones, if you will.

In this novel, a man and a woman—a former couple, and a marriage of true minds, though they never technically marry— look back and take stock of how the circumstances in their lives changed. This was also my state of mind as I began translating *Trust* in Princeton, New Jersey, in the spring of 2020. Until then, I kept hoping that the "novel coronavirus" was a fleeting term, and thus a fleeting problem. I kept assuming that my son, who had been living and studying in Rome until he abruptly boarded a plane for JFK the day after Italy went into national lockdown, would soon enough fly back to finish high school with his classmates. I assumed my husband and daughter and I would fly to Rome, too, to celebrate his graduation. When I realized that none of this was going to happen, I turned to Starnone's Italian instead. I printed out one page each day to make the experience last. The irony of translating this novel just as our day-to-day lives had changed overnight was not lost on me. And there was another layer of irony I appreciated, one that involves Starnone's impeccably accurate and hilarious description of the vicissitudes of being a writer, and of publishing, from one book to the next—from composing to editing to reviewing proofs to traveling to sleeping in hotels to speaking in rooms full of people to signing copies to going out to dinner afterward—all of which I recognized, some of which I have had the pleasure of doing in Starnone's company, and much of which neither he nor I could any longer do.

The play of substitution can be distilled into the sentence I love most in this novel, in which an open umbrella, blown by a sudden gust of wind, turns "from a cupola into a cup." It is a stroke of genius. In Italian, *mutare da cupola in calice* means literally, to change from a cupola into a chalice. What Starnone evokes here is a change of form, both visually and linguistically. But the wordplay (I'll be so bold to say) is even more satisfying in English. The sentence doesn't end, however, with the progression from cupola to cup. It continues: "How easy it is for words to change the shape of things" (*"com'è facile cambiare a parole la forma delle cose"*). That *forma* takes us straight back to Ovid, and to the opening words of the *Metamorphoses*: "In nova fert animus mutatas dicere formas / corpora" ("My soul is inclined to speak of forms altered into new bodies"). Ovid's verb *dicere* ("to speak") also echoes Starnone's pithy first line, which poses as a question: "Amore, che dire?" ("Love, what to say?"). Starnone may be a builder of roller coasters, but he is also a master of the backward glance, and his ferocious tales are always tempered by a keening spirit that harks back to Greek and Latin elegy, but also has the universal resonance of popular lyric. Paul McCartney put it this way: "I said something wrong, now I long for yesterday." Think of that line when you think back on themes of language and love in this novel.

During the pandemic year that I have spent in the company of this novel, my understanding of *invece* changed just like an umbrella in the wind, from an everyday workhorse in my Italian vocabulary to a lexical distillation of pure poetry and philosophy. From book to book, this type of revelation is what translating my friend's work has taught me about language and about words—that they change as we blink and that they are rich with alternatives. It is my engagement with Starnone's texts over the past six years that has rendered me, definitively, a translator, and this novel activity in my creative life has rendered clear the inherent instability not only of language but of life, which is why, in undertaking the task of choosing English words to take the place of his Italian ones, I am ever thankful and forever changed.

PRINCETON, 2021

(8)

Traduzione (stra)ordinaria/ (Extra)ordinary translation

On Gramsci

On January 31, 2021, Silvio Pons, a historian and the director of the Gramsci Institute Foundation in Rome, sent me an email asking if I would like to say say a few words in spring, over Zoom, to celebrate the new and definitive Italian edition of Antonio Gramsci's *Letters from Prison* recently published by Einaudi. Gramsci began writing them after he was arrested on November 8, 1926, by Italy's Fascist government. He was initially placed in solitary confinement in Rome's Regina Coeli prison, and subsequently transferred several times to a series of other prisons and places of confinement throughout Italy. He died in a clinic in Rome on April 27, 1937, six days after his prison sentence expired and two days after suffering a cerebral hemorrhage.

I already knew these details about Gramsci. When I am in Rome and walk past Regina Coeli in Trastevere, I think of him. I have stood more than once before his final resting place in the non-Catholic cemetery in Testaccio, located just a short walk across the river from my apartment. But when Silvio Pons wrote to me I was far from Rome, and teaching a virtual translation course to a group of undergraduate students in Princeton, New Jersey.

It should come as no surprise that immersing myself in the day-to-day reality and reflections of a man who was internally exiled and incarcerated for eleven years, separated from family, friends, and the world at large for his political beliefs, has altered my own perception of the months—eleven, when I began keeping these notes—of restrictions and limited human interactions due to a global pandemic. But a dedicated and methodical reading of Gramsci's letters over a period of two months surprised me for other reasons. For, though I knew that Gramsci was born and raised in Sardinia, and was a founder and former leader of the Italian Communist Party, and lives on, more than eight decades later, as a Marxist icon, it was only thanks to engaging with his letters during the pandemic that I came to regard him, and now revere him, also as an icon of translation.

IL TASCABILE / THE PAPERBACK

Silvio Pons sent me a pdf of the volume: it contained 489 letters, a significant critical apparatus, and numbered 1,262 pages. I also had another, less comprehensive version of the letters, a paperback of less than 300 pages. I had acquired the latter volume in Italy, attracted by a preface written by Michela Murgia. Back then, I was motivated by curiosity about Gramsci the writer as opposed to the political philosopher. I was eager to hear, in untranslated form, his voice, and to learn a bit about his personal life in his own words. I remember traveling with the book in my purse and pulling it out to read when I was on a bus or tram or waiting room in Rome. Leafing through the letters from time to time, skipping around, I crossed a border to read words he had never intended for me to encounter. On the other side of that border I discovered a warm, witty, astonishingly intelligent, curious, and well-read man whose observations kept me company while I was on the go. I was struck by his talent for describing everyday scenes and actions, his subjectivity, his sincerity. I was swept up in a tragic narrative that was also full of vitality and intimacy, one that interrogated life and ideas on every page. It felt like a complex novel I could dip in and out of, that was always inviting. At a certain point the book changed location; I decided to bring it to Princeton on one of my numerous trips back and forth between Italy and the US—maybe I'd wanted to read it during the plane ride? In any case, I placed it by the side of my bed, to accompany me now and then on that nightly border-crossing between wakefulness and sleep. It now strikes me more than ever that while I first discovered Gramsci's letters when I was moving from one place to another, my second discovery, sitting in Firestone Library at Princeton during COVID-19, occurred in an historic moment characterized by stillness. These two distinct modes of reading correspond to the richly contradictory nature of Gramsci's letters from prison: they are words, always moving from place, written by a man who could go nowhere.

VIAGGIO DI TRADUZIONE / TRANSLATION JOURNEY

In a letter from December 19, 1926, from the island of Ustica, Gramsci wrote to his sister-in-law Tania Schucht: "È stato questo il pezzo più brutto del viaggio di traduzione / That was the worst part of my translation journey."[1] Or so it seemed to me. Until

---

[1] Translations from Gramsci's letters are my own.

then I did not know that *traduzione*, the word for "translation" in Italian, has a second meaning: it is a bureaucratic term which refers to the transportation of individuals who are under suspicion or detained. The discovery of this second meaning both bewildered and amazed me. How, after my own intense study of Italian, and my own relationship with the activity and teaching of translation, could I not have known this? I began to think of both prisoners and language in transit, on the same ontological spectrum. In the letter of December 19, Gramsci recounts, in minute detail, his movements from one place to another: a sequence involving handcuffs, prison automobile to the port, boat, vaporetto, a series of ladders, third-class cabin, wrists tied as part of a chain gang, and his final destination: his cell. He is aware of each moment of transition, every shift. The memory of these movements is underscored, of course, by his enforced immobility. Further ahead, he notes: "Non possiamo oltrepassare determinati limiti / We cannot go past certain limits." The point of all that moving (for his captors) was, in the end, a condition of not moving, or moving in a constrained, monitored way. Gramsci arrived at Ustica thanks to a voyage of translation. The following eleven years were to be a voyage of translation of another kind.

I DIZIONARI E LE GRAMMATICHE /
DICTIONARIES AND GRAMMARS

Part of the reality of Gramsci's imprisonment was an ongoing request, in the letters, for certain essential objects, including clothing, items for personal hygiene, and medicines. But essential items for Gramsci also meant books, both Italian and in translation, and among the books a steady stream of foreign dictionaries and grammars representing his profound relationship to other languages. As soon as he gets to Ustica, on December 9, 1926, he requests "subito, se puoi / immediately, if you can," a German and Russian grammar, and a German dictionary. In outlining his prison routine, he lists, as his second priority (the first is to stay in good health) the intention to study German and Russian "con metodo e continuità / methodically and consistently." He asks Tania again for the German and Russian Berlitz on December 19. On May 23, he reiterates that his linguistic studies remain his principal focus. He asks for more dictionaries, mentioning that one was lost. "Sono proprio deciso di fare dello studio delle lingue la mia occupazione predominante / I've really made up my mind to make language study my predominant activity." He goes on to say that he intends to more carefully study (after Russian and German) English, Spanish, Portuguese, and Romanian, all of which he has merely "studiacchiato / cursorily studied" in school and at university. This intensified pursuit of language-learning is what enables him to maintain his equilibrium psychologically in prison. By December 1929, in one of the most moving passages of the letters, he says that his spirits are not flagging *because* of language, since the study of language is his salvation: "Il mio stato d'animo è tale che se anche fossi condannato a morte, continuerei a essere tranquillo e anche la sera prima dell'esecuzione magari studierei una lezione di lingua cinese / My state of mind is such that, even if I were sentenced to death, I would continue to feel calm and even the evening before my execution perhaps I'd have a Chinese language lesson."

STUDI E VIAGGI / STUDIES AND TRAVELS

Translation was a reality, aspiration, discipline, anchor, and metaphor for Gramsci throughout his life; it merely intensified once he was arrested and imprisoned. As a student he read (and thus translated) Ancient Greek and Latin literature. The list of other languages he learned as a student includes French, German, English, and Sanskrit. He also studied linguistics and dialects. His profound engagement with Italian literature already represented a relationship with a language that was distinct from the language of his native Sardinia, where he lived until the age of twenty. Such was his identification with alternative linguistic systems that he published his early articles under the pseudonym Alfa Gamma, formed by the Greek letters that correspond to his initials. At a certain point, he also picked up Russian. As he transformed from a student of literature to a journalist in his early twenties—though in fact he remained a zealous student of literature all his life—his knowledge of other languages was crucial to both his political formation and his editorial vision, enabling him to publish writings by Lenin and Marx in the magazines he collaborated on, and positioning him to take part in the broader, international, inherently multilingual conversation of communism itself. His translation of Stalin and others under Fascism underscores the essential and subversive role translation has always played. All translation is a political act, but especially so under Mussolini, who, with his ideology of linguistic purity, was opposed to everything the act of translation entails, advocates, and signifies, and strictly censored and surveilled the publication of literature in translation under the regime. Gramsci's growing exposure to Russian and German, two crucial languages for his understanding of communist practice and philosophy, was no doubt enhanced by his travels to Moscow in 1922, and to Germany and Austria the year after that. Though he does not speak very much about his travels in the letters, he shares memories of his former studies and mentions Matteo Bartoli, his linguistics professor in Turin, who also became a friend.

MATRIMONIO / MARRIAGE

A translation may be understood as a marriage between texts: an intimate and, one hopes, everlasting bond. Gramsci married into translation quite literally. In Russia, in 1922, the same year that Mussolini came to power following his March on Rome, Gramsci met Giulia Apollonova Schucht. Born to Russian parents, Giulia spent her childhood in Switzerland and in Rome but returned to live in Russia by the time she was nearly twenty. When Gramsci went to visit the city of Ivanov Voznesensk as a member of the Presidium of the Communist International, she served as his interpreter. Together they worked on a translation of a novel by Aleksandr Bogdanov. In 1923 they were married, at which point translation became a permanent part of Gramsci's personal life, family relations, and future.

DOPPIA IDENTITÀ / DOUBLE IDENTITY

Gramsci was and will always be more than one thing. He was both Sardinian and Italian, both a politician and a linguist.[2] And, though he was confined for eleven years, he remained in constant communication with others. Like Primo Levi—not only a chemist-writer but a writer of many identities and iterations— Gramsci was a polyhedric figure. And yet, the flip side of a double (or plural) identity can be a lack of identity. In a long letter on October 12, 1931, Gramsci talks to Tania about the question of language and race, and specifically about the Jewish condition (his mother-in-law came from a Jewish family; the first racial laws, promulgated in Italy in 1938, were still a ways off). "Una 'razza' che ha dimenticato la sua lingua antica significa già che

---

[2] Though he says to Giulia on May 20, 1929, that he is only "half Sardinian" and not an "authentic one."

ha perduto la maggior parte dell'eredità del passato, della prima concezione del mondo che ha assorbito la cultura (con la lingua) di un popolo conquistatore: cosa significa dunque più 'razza?' in questo caso? / A 'race' that has forgotten its ancient language means that it has already lost most of its legacy of the past, and of the first concept of the world that has absorbed the culture (along with the language) of a conquering people: what, then, does race means anymore, in this case?" He later declares in this same letter, "io stesso non ho nessuna razza / I myself have no race." He speaks of his Albanian father, his grandmother's Spanish blood, and adds that his relationship to his Italian identity is one that is forged: a dynamic process of becoming Italian that grows out of migration, of movement— of "translation" in one of its truest senses. Though he concludes toward the end of the letter that his culture is "fundamentally Italian" and that he did not feel "dilaniato tra due mondi / torn between two worlds," I believe it is the very lack of precise roots, and of language, combined with his insatiable thirst for new languages, that gives rise to and sustains Gramsci the translator. And perhaps his intrinsically layered identity also drove him to create relationships with others like him. Both Tania and Giulia, for example, worked as translators and interpreters, in embassies and other environments that required them to be perpetually on the border, negotiating between languages. They, like he, were hybrid individuals, each with a hybrid consciousness. I was struck by this line on September 7, 1931, to Tania—"Così mi diverto da me stesso / So I entertain myself"— indicating his two halves, or his dual spirit. There is an interesting echo on November 9, 1931, when he talks about the practice of splitting matches with a needle—a prison habit—in order to make two from one: "Per i fiammiferi vale la pratica carceraria di scindere, con un ago, ogni fiammifero in due parti, raddoppiandoli / For matches, we have the prisoner's habit of doubling them by splitting each in two parts with a needle."

DOPPIO TESTO / DOUBLE TEXT

Gramsci's literary production in prison was divided between the massive number of letters and the massive number of notebooks. The meaning of each body of work is augmented by a reading of the other. They are two texts in conversation, and conversation is the basis of any translation. He began writing in his notebooks on February 8, 1929. About two months later, on April 22, he writes to Tania, "tra gli studi più proficui è certo quello delle lingue moderne; basta una grammatica, che si può trovare anche nelle bancarelle dei libri usati per pochissimi soldi / among the most fruitful studies is certainly that of modern languages; all you need is a grammar, which you can find even in a used-book stall for very little money." And a few sentences later: "Tuttavia io credo che un carcerato politico deve cavar sangue anche da una rapa. Tutto consiste nel dare un fine alle proprie letture e saper prendere appunti [se si ha il permesso di scrivere] / Nevertheless, I believe that a political prisoner needs to extract blood even from a stone: it's all a matter of giving purpose to one's reading and knowing how to take notes [assuming that one has writing privileges]." He is already commenting on the writing of the notebooks. The notebook entries are provisional, fragmentary; private jottings that will be elaborated and further articulated. Within the notebooks, certain ideas are elaborated over and over. The letters feel more coherent, contained, structured. If the notebook entries are in some sense forbidding (though utterly fascinating) in that they are diaristic, more interior, the letters, also interior, are a form of narrative that points outward and, indeed, may be read as an unfolding story, as drama. The letters are always crossing the border and responding to outside voices, to an awareness and longing for the other. It is in the letters, and only in the letters, and then only rarely, that he exposes his intense isolation, vulnerability, and desperation. The strange effect of reading the letters is that, in hearing only what Gramsci writes but not what he receives in return, we experience only a single strand of a double thread.

PATERNITÀ ATTRAVERSO LE PAROLE / FATHERHOOD THROUGH WORDS

It is thanks principally to language in the form of letter-writing that Gramsci is a father. He had little contact with Delio, born in Moscow, and he never saw Giuliano. They lived in Russia and wrote to him in Russian. It is only in correspondence that he shares memories and other pieces of his past with them. It is only in letters that he is able establish a connection with them. And yet, language poses an additional barrier. Both Giulia and Tania serve as key figures—as translators—so that Gramsci can communicate with his sons. On March 26, 1927, he notes proudly that Delio has begun to speak his mother's language, Russian, and remarks that he also knows Italian and sings in French without getting confused. Previously in that same letter, he asks Tania what language her own children speak, and encourages her to allow them to speak in Sardinian, believing that is was a mistake not to teach his niece, Edmea, to speak in Sardinian, defined here not as a dialect but as its own language. The relationship between father and child, Gramsci observes, is one of give-and-take between generations, and thus of another type of movement. On June 15, 1931, he tells his mother: "Ogni nostra azione si trasmette negli altri secondo il suo valore, di bene e di male, passa di padre in figlio, da una generazione all'altra in un movimento perpetuo / Each of our actions is transmitted in others according to its value of good and bad, passing from father to son, from one generation to the next in perpetual motion." There is that crucial word again, *motion*. Gramsci's letters to and about Delio and Giuliano exemplify his devotion for them, but his absence from his sons' lives afflicts him from the very beginning. In one of the first letters from Regina Coeli prison, he writes to Giulia, "Le mie responsabilità di genitore serio mi tormentano / My responsibilities as a conscientious parent torment me." But as the children grow older, the language questions grows more problematic. A year before his life ended, on November 5, 1936, he writes again to Giulia, hoping that she will be able to translate his letters to their children, whom he never got to know, "per 'tradurre' non letteralmente, ma secondo le loro mentalità, i miei biglietti a loro, per aiutarmi a comprendere loro intimamente / to 'translate,' not literally, but according to their mentality, my notes to them, to help me understand them intimately." At times he signs off after writing to his sons with the affectionate term "babbo" (meaning "dad"). At times he signs his letters, even to his sons, "Antonio." As loving and persistent as his letters to his sons are, the prevailing sentiment is one of acute frustration, and of feeling like a ghost in their lives. On December 14, 1931, to Tania, he feels incapable of having a relationship with his sons because he knows nothing about them, and cannot participate in their lives: "La verità è che sono proprio incapace psicologicamente di mettermi in relazione con loro perché concretamente conosco nulla della loro vita e del loro sviluppo / The truth is that I really am incapable, psychologically, of having a relationship with them because I essentially know nothing about their lives, their development." Toward the end of the letter he says he fears that his sons regard him as a Flying Dutchman, and then asks: "Come potrebbe scrivere

l'Olandese volante / How might the Flying Dutchman write?"
A Flying Dutchman is a ghost ship destined to sail the seas forever, to be in eternal transit. He adds, "Mi ripugna il mestiere
di fantasma / My calling as a ghost repels me." In identifying
with this image, Gramsci complicates the question of identity
even further and, presaging perhaps his own end, becomes the
vehicle as well as the subject of translation.

RAPPORTO / RELATIONSHIP

A translation implies a relationship that is at once intimate
and imperfect between two texts, notions, realities, moments.
Reading Gramsci's letters, one understands how his personal
relationships—with his wife, mother, sister-in-law, brother,
children, and others—are also both intimate and imperfect.
Reading Gramsci's letters, one realizes that every interpersonal
relationship can be read as a form of translation.

LA SECONDA LETTURA / THE SECOND READING

As I've said, the second encounter with the letters has been
very different from the first. I knew I had two months to prepare for the event for the Gramsci Foundation, and I wanted
to read as many of the letters as I could before then. I set aside
time each day, switching between the massive pdf on-screen
and the worn-out paperback I recuperated from my shelves.
During the second reading I began to underline passages and
to take notes. I began reserving time at Princeton's Firestone
Library to absorb the letters, alone and undisturbed. I wanted
to read them in order, systematically, one after the next.

ECO / ECHO

I have proposed, elsewhere, that echoes are one way to reflect
on the act and consequence of translation. Certainly there
are passages in the letters and the notebooks that echo one

another; if read side by side, one detects moments when Gramsci argues and interprets similar things different ways. But by now I detect other echoes, yes, between Gramsci's confinement and certain aspects of my life during the pandemic. How happy he would have been, here in this library full of books, where I read him and think of him. At a certain point in my reading something happens. I must read them daily, I must come to the library daily to read them. I must walk from my home to the library, sit at the same table, and occasionally move to the same chair. And I must be within walking distance, in the library, of the various dictionaries, especially Salvatore Battaglia's twenty-one-volume *Grande dizionario della lingua italiana* (referred to hereafter as the Battaglia), which helps me understand the letters once certain words begin to require deeper investigation. The more I read him the more I must read him, and the more I grow aware of the freedom of moving back and forth between my home and the library the more I think about the full meaning of the word *traduzione*. My time slots are specific: due to the pandemic one must check in and leave at the appointed times. There are new rules to follow: only one person at a time in the restroom; water fountains and certain seats blocked off with tape. These are petty restrictions compared to the infinite freedom I experience every time I enter this library and find over 7 million books, potentially, at my disposal. How many physical volumes, I wonder, kept Gramsci company in his various cells?

ORIGINALE / ORIGINAL

This word, part of a translator's lexicon for good or for ill, is also a word to define Gramsci's unique literary and intellectual output. *Originale*/original, from the Latin *origo*, meaning origin, roots us to beginnings, to the act of coming into being, to founding myths, to the places in which we begin, to our parents and ancestors, to where narratives emerge and to the sources from which words derive. But an origin also gives rise to a point of departure. The highly original work of Gramsci has spawned translations, not just "literal" translations from one language to another but meaningful heuristic offshoots in the form of scholarly analysis, all of which underscores the fact that translation describes the process of one text that becomes many.

LETTURA DAL CARCERE / PRISON READING

Translinguistic themes and concerns were an ongoing theme in Gramsci's reading life. We know he read Marx in French and that he made annotations on Esperanto and on the role of the vernacular. He devotes pages, in the notebooks as well as the letters, to his readings of Croce and Machiavelli, of Dostoevsky and of G. K. Chesterton. His reading of Canto X of Dante's *Inferno* is an analysis of a scene in which the action revolves around verb tenses, issues of miscommunication, silences, and the unsaid. His reading of Manzoni revisits the question of Italy's national language. The intensity of Gramsci's thinking in general reveals a mind that repeatedly visits his subjects, that reads with a level of intensity and scrutiny that translation inevitably demands. I would go so far as to say that Gramsci read everything *as* a translator, whether he intended to translate it or not. Like most discerning multilingual readers, Gramsci has a lot to say about translated work. On August 26, 1929 (the year he received formal permission to write, and began the notebooks), he writes to Tania extensively and explicitly about translation, and complains about poor translations in particular. He goes into detail, drawing on examples of both French and Latin texts, and criticizes a version of Tacitus translated by the Futurist Marinetti.

TRADUZIONE DELLE LETTERE /
TRANSLATION OF THE LETTERS

There is an ongoing need for his letters to be translated, mostly
out of Italian into Russian and vice versa. On March 19, 1927,
he tells Tania to ask his mother-in-law to send him a long letter
either in Italian or in French, and in this same letter he speaks
of deepening his university thesis, a study of comparative literature, and uses the German *für ewig* ("forever") to describe
his intentions. This is just one example of the many non-Italian
words and phrases woven throughout the letters. In fact, Gramsci's letters will need to be translated for any reader who does
not know all the languages that appear in them—all the languages he knew and incorporated in his writing. In addition
to the Russian words that crop up, especially in his letters to
Delio and Giuliano, and the Sardinian terms he writes about to
his mother and others, I came across the English words *thermos*
and *schooners*, as well as *mneme* from the Greek for memory,
and *échaffaudage*, which means scaffolding in French. Reading
the letters, I learned new Italian words including *zufolare*, another way of saying whistle, which Gramsci uses to describe
the sound that would ideally be produced were Giuliano and
Delio to know how to skip stones on the water (May 18, 1931).

TRADUZIONE NELLE LETTERE /
TRANSLATION IN THE LETTERS

We know that among the thirty-odd notebooks Gramsci wrote
while in captivity, some were devoted entirely to translation.
But Gramsci also writes in the letters about words and their
meanings, that is to say, about translation issues. On January 18,
1932, to his sister Teresina, he refers to his own translation "per

esercizio / as an exercise" from German of Grimms' fairy tales, which he produces "come un mio contributo allo sviluppo della fantasia dei piccoli / as a contribution of mine to the development of the fantasy of the little ones."

TRASLITTERARE / TRANSLITERATE

In Battaglia, the word that immediately follows *traslazione* is *trasletterante* (transliterator), after which comes *traslitterare* (transliterate). We find examples of Gramsci's tendency to transliterate throughout the letters: letters to Delio and Giuliano, for example, are sometimes signed "Papa" in Cyrillic script. On May 20, 1929, he signs off in a letter to Delio "Toi papa," which is an imperfect transliteration from the Russian *tvoj papa*, meaning "your father" (in Italian, *tuo papà*). He signs a letter to Delio on April 8, 1935, among the last he wrote, directly in Russian: Твой папа.

TRADUZIONE NEI QUADERNI / TRANSLATION IN THE NOTEBOOKS

In the notebooks, Gramsci talks of translation as a dialectical process, as a means of communication with the proletariat, and thus as a form of revolution. Two examples of Gramsci's own translation in the notebooks are worth mentioning here in extreme synthesis: 1) his first use of the word *translation*, in the first notebook, speaking of the Risorgimento and of Ferrari's inability to "translate" French into Italian; and 2) his own mistranslations of Lenin in the seventh notebook: "Non abbiamo capito come 'tradurre' nelle lingue 'europee' la nostra lingua / We have not understood how to 'translate' our language in the 'European' languages" is actually "non abbiamo capito come si deve mettere la nostra esperienza russa alla portata degli stranieri / We have not understood how to put our Russian experiences into the hands of foreigners." One might reflect at length on the fascinating substitutions and choices here.

INTERPRETAZIONI / INTERPRETATIONS

As an accompaniment to my study of the letters, I begin to skim the immense scholarship that addresses Gramsci's relationship to language. At the library, I read articles in both English and Italian regarding linguistic and cultural diversity in relation to his political theories. As I accumulate notes on Gramsci's approach to (and engagement with) language, a potential course comes to mind: a translation course dedicated entirely to Gramsci, who was both a theorist and practitioner of translation. The idea for this essay also comes to mind. Interpretation—which is most of what translation is—also plays a role in his lengthy reflections on the meaning and method of psychoanalysis, the interpretation of the past, of memory and of dreams. Gramsci, to me, is an impressive interpreter of maladies; many of the letters are detailed explanations of his considerable and complicated and persistent physical ailments.

FOTOGRAFIE / PHOTOGRAPHS

Throughout the letters I was moved by the careful interpretation of the photos. Gramsci recognizes the growth of his sons by means of pictures as well as words. The letter to Giulia on January 13, 1931, contains a lengthy reflection on five pictures that serve to bridge the separation he endures: "Sono le fotografie più interessanti che ho ricevuto in questi quattro anni e mezzo dopo il distacco da te e dai nostri figliolini / They are the most interesting photographs I have received in these four and a half years after being separated from you and our little children."

When he requests photos, he asks for his sons' heights and weights on the back. He wants, from the photos, a "concrete sense" of them as opposed to his imaginings: "mi aiutano ad immaginare un po' più concretamente la vostra vita e a fantasticare meno / they help me to imagine your life a little more concretely and to invent less" (August 1, 1932). I read this careful reading of images, which also results in meaning, as another form of translation.

DIFFERENZA ED EQUIVALENZA / DIFFERENCE AND EQUIVALENCE

Gramsci, who meditates on the mysterious evolution of words throughout the letters, is preoccupied by how things are said in other languages. A letter from May 18, 1931, contains a long reflection on the Italian use of words like *happy* and *good* and *beautiful*. He ties these expressions to culture and to wishful thinking (the Italian term is *velleità*), concluding: "la vita reale non può essere mai determinata da suggerimenti ambientali o da formule, ma nasce da radici interiori / real life can never be determined by environmental factors or formulas, but is born from interior roots." The question of difference and equivalence in language is ongoing for the translator. We search for equivalents, knowing fully that, given the difference between one language and another, no true equivalent exists. The whole of Gramsci's prison correspondence reinforces the crucial fact that he is different from everyone he writes to; that he is incarcerated and they are not.

DIALETTO / DIALECT

The letters contain numerous references and digressions on Gramsci's thinking about questions of language and power in a time when the Italian national language was being extolled. But on November 17, 1930, he tells Tatiana that a "double language" persists, and continues to exist: the language of the people as opposed to the learned language of intellectuals. This language of the people is dialect (opposed by Mussolini) as opposed to "official" Italian.

SARDO / SARDINIAN

Gramsci's letters to his mother are full of questions and reflections in Sardinian, a Romance language closely related to non-classical Latin and incorporating Arabic, Byzantine Greek, Ligurian, Catalan, and Spanish influences. The Sardinian language binds Gramsci to his mother, to his origins. On December 15, 1930, when he observes, to his mother, that five years have passed since he has been imprisoned, he uses a Sardinian expression to describe his condition, writing, "e sono sicuro che se anche non posso più 'zaccurrare sa fae arrostia' tuttavia non proverei dispiacere a vedere e sentire gli altri a 'zaccurrare' / and I am sure that even if I can no longer 'zaccurrare fae arrostia' [shell the roasted favas], nevertheless, I wouldn't mind seeing and hearing that others do."

NOMI E ANIMALI / NAMES AND ANIMALS

In inventing new names, in declining them, Gramsci is transforming identity, reinforcing his affection for those he loves. The playful (and subversive) act of renaming is one form of overturning, of questioning language and identity in its most essentially linked form. Renaming is a form of translation and also a form of love. Thus Giulia becomes Julka, Julca, Iulca; Giuliano Iulik; Delio turns into Delca and Delka; and Tatiana into Tania, Tatanca, Tataniska, Tatanička. Nonhuman creatures constitute a fascinating thread in the letters and could easily be the subject of a separate essay. In a letter of February 8, 1932, he tells Tania to include, in parentheses, the names in Russian for the birds and fish to which he refers in a letter to Delio. He adds that Giulia has not been able to translate, properly, his Italian. Though acknowledging that some of the creatures may be untranslatable, he insists on distinguishing a *scricciolo* (wren) for an *aquila* (eagle). Not only is Gramsci attentive to the names of certain animals, he thinks about how to communicate with them. The letters he writes to Delio are full of references to animals such as elephants, parrots, dogs. On February 22, 1932, he talks at length about the pets Delio is keeping. On June 1, 1931, he recounts (for Delio) a Sardinian fable that involves a talking mouse. At one point the names of animals bring up the ongoing question of dialect: on June 2, 1930, he writes to Tatiana of his memory of a lizard called a "scruzone" which, in school, his natural history teacher tells him is imaginary, insisting that the creature was a country superstition. When this memory returns to him in prison, he shares it with Tania, and he asks her to look up the Italian name of the species to confirm whether is it related to the French "seps" he finds in Larousse. Gramsci has particular respect for veterinarians because "guariscono animali che non parlano e non possono descrivere i sintomi del loro male / they heal animals who cannot speak to describe the symptoms of their illness" (September 7, 1931). That is to say, their cure transcends language. Interested throughout the letters in regional cooking, and in the names of specific Sardinian dishes and recipes, he tells Giulia on August 31, 1931, that his sons must learn to distinguish between comestible and noncomestible frogs, and sends detailed instructions for how to fry the comestible variety.

CONVERSAZIONE E COMUNICAZIONE /
CONVERSATION AND COMMUNICATION

What I read, in the letters, was only one side of a conversation. But what I learned was just how crucial conversation and communication were for Gramsci. As I mentioned, the letters and the notebooks are in conversation with each other. If one is a monologue, the other is an intended dialogue. One is a type of diary or letter to oneself. The other is a correspondence with various individuals. But the letters are also internal conversations, ruminations, and intellectual explorations, conversations as much with himself as with others. What is pointed inward is vast and global, while what is outward is often intensely personal. They must be read together: in many ways, one is the translation of the other.

AVANTI E INDIETRO / BACK AND FORTH

We can think of translation as a back-and-forth, and we can detect this in very real terms as the letters are sent off and arrive, and packages are received, or not. It is the back-and-forth of language across time and space that sustains him.

RECIPROCITÀ / RECIPROCITY

His state of mind in prison is in direct correlation to the response to his letters. On August 3, 1931, Giulia's silences, in particular, plague him and exacerbate the acute separation he feels. On November 30, 1931, his anxiety is that "non so niente di te ... non riesco a immaginare nulla della tua vita / I know nothing about you ... I can't imagine anything about your life." They have become ghosts, unreal beings, to one another. He complains of the vagueness of her letters. Unable to touch her, he writes that he would like to be able to shake her firmly, violently, even at the risk of being wrongful and wicked with her.

What he seeks above all is a response to his anguish. On October 6, 1930, he complains to Giulia: "Non siamo mai riusciti a intavolare un 'dialogo': le nostre lettere sono una serie di 'monologhi' che non sempre riescono ad accordarsi / We've never managed to establish a 'dialogue': our letters are only a series of 'monologues' that don't always manage to match up."

DEFINIZIONI / DEFINITIONS

In reflecting upon certain words in prison, Gramsci gave us a new vocabulary. Though he did not invent words like *hegemony* and *praxis*, he revised our understanding of them, redefined them, and caused them to circulate and to resonate differently. He translates and transforms these terms, with their Ancient Greek roots, by means of reading and reinterpreting them.

MUTAMENTO / MUTATION

In the letter of September 20, 1931, as he lays down his thoughts on Canto X of Dante's *Inferno*, Gramsci talks about language that changes, a fact that generates the activity of translation throughout history. It is the very fact of language as something that is always changing, always becoming something else, that instigates, necessitates, and perpetuates the act of translation. This also explains why translation is the underpinning of revolution.

DECLINAZIONI / DECLINATIONS

As a student first of Ancient Greek and Latin and then of German and Russian, Gramsci was thinking and reading across multiple declined languages, that is, languages in which the form of a word is always changing based on syntactical demands. And if we decline, more generally, the word *translation*? Gramsci did, whether consciously or not. The cases correspond not to nominative, genitive, and so forth, but to a series of valences of which linguistic is only the first, followed by cultural, historical, philosophical, political, and, I would argue, also emotional.

ORDINE / ORDER

Gramsci wrote about systems because he understood them and thought about how to go about changing them. As a free man, he wrote for a review called *Ordine nuovo* [A new order], a publication dedicated to "creating an Italian equivalent of the Russian 'soviets.'" If we focus on language, we see that languages are ordered systems, and that they are bound by rules. Tullio De Mauro speaks of Gramsci's systematic thinking in the notebooks, and says they appear fragmentary only because they are written in prison under the Fascist system. Instead he points to their profound analytical rigor. In the letters of August 3, 1931, Gramsci speaks of his "l'abito di severa disciplina filologica / habit of severe philological discipline" acquired at university which has given him "un'eccessiva, forse, provvista di scrupoli metodici / perhaps an excess supply of methodical scruples." It is this strict discipline that sustains him and enables him to produce as much as he did. On February 22, 1922, Gramsci requests notebooks of a specific kind so that his jottings don't turn muddled, as his aim is to "obtain a certain intellectual order." The word *ordine*, which is never far from any conversation about hegemony, is of course linked to the adjective *ordinario*/ordinary, of which I have already spoken. In Battaglia, the word *ordine* runs across fourteen pages and has one hundred separate definitions. Order characterizes the rational mind, and may have been in Gramsci's mind when he spoke apprehensively of Giulia, who "combatte contro fantasmi suscitati dalla sua fantasia disordinata e febbrile / battles with ghosts aroused by her disorderly, febrile fantasy" (February 15, 1932).

SILENZIO / SILENCE

December 12, 1927, to his mother: "L'assenza di notizie diventa qualche volta un vero tormento / The absence of news becomes, at times, a real torment." Silence also surrounds the mental illness of his wife, which is never referred to explicitly in the letters. Nor is the reality of his twenty-year sentence. The word *fascism* is never mentioned. Everything he wrote was, needless to say, in the hands of censors. One of the tragic threads of the letters is his inability to understand Giulia's letters. "Cerco il bandolo della matassa / I look for the crux of the matter," he writes to Tania on February 15, 1932. Mental illness was, then especially, also a case of untranslatability. At times he is the one to withhold information. On May 23, 1932, for example: "Certe cose mi dispiace scriverle in una lettera carceraria / There are certain things I don't like to write in a prison letter."

VOCE / VOICE

What makes the letters a great work of literature is the complexity of the voice. And though they can be read as a sustained first-person novel, in fact that voice changes from letter to letter depending on whom he writes to and when, shifting from irony to sincerity, from light to dark, from recipes to philosophy, from matter-of-fact concerns to haunting reflections. This fluctuation is especially striking when he writes to different people on the same day. This would be the greatest challenge, for the translator: to give voice, in another language, to each of these individual voices.

CONFINE-CONFINO / CONFINE-CONFINEMENT

These two key terms for Gramsci—let's call them fraternal if not identical twins—emerge from the Italian verb *confinare*, which has two meanings in Italian. One is intransitive, the other is transitive. The intransitive *confinare* means to share a common border, or confine. The transitive version means to send someone away, to an isolated place, as a form of punishment. This second sense can also be conveyed with the expression *mandare al confino*. In Italian, then, the line running between one territory from another—and, by extension, one language from another—refers also to a penal act by means of distancing. The root of *confinare* is *con + fines* (from the Latin *cum + fines*: with limits, i.e., setting bounds). I expected the Italian *confinare* to come from the same verb in Latin, but it doesn't. In ancient Rome, when someone was banished or exiled, the only transitive verb was *relegare*, to relegate; but Cicero uses combinations of nouns and verbs, such as "exagere in exsilium," or "pellere/expellere in exsilium," or "mittere in exsilium," or "eicere in exsilium" (all variations of "drive into exile"). The equivalent of *confinare* in the sense of "have a confine in common" in Latin is *adiacere*, meaning "to lie next to or border upon," giving us the word *adjacent*. The transitive, punitive *confinare* in Italian emerges under Fascism, and is the verb that describes and defines Gramsci's state as he writes his letters and fills his notebooks. This word may have been Gramsci's fate, but it was also his liberation. He is sent *al confino*, though the Latin *confinis* is a word that both divides and unites. The Latin *confinis* (as well as the related terms *confine* and *confinium*) all point to a common border, to relationships of contiguousness and closeness and kinship, just as we see in these letters. In other words, that which separates also represents proximity. Gramsci, in a state of exile, by means of letters and nothing else, is a father, a husband, a brother-in-law, and a son. The letters create and maintain connection, even as they emphasize his isolation. Gramsci contradicted his confinement through language, resisting it by always communicating and with the

staggering amount of scholarly writing he produced. His febrile intellectual activity while in captivity, and the scope of
his thought, can best be described in Italian with the privative
sconfinato: literally, lacking confines, or boundless.

TRADUTTORE / TRANSLATOR

Gramsci gives a great deal of advice to both Giulia and Tania
regarding the importance of producing translations, and of
being a translator. On September 5, 1932, he encourages Giulia to become a more dedicated and qualified translator out of
Italian. For Gramsci, this means moving beyond commercial
correspondence and journalistic prose toward "la capacità di
tradurre qualsiasi autore, sia letterato, o politico, o storico o
filosofo / the ability to translate any author, whether literary
or political, whether an historian or a philosopher." He tells
her—and us—of the value of this work, that which pertains to
an ideal translator: "cioè un tale traduttore dovrebbe conoscere
criticamente due civiltà ed essere in grado di far conoscere l'una
all'altra servendosi del linguaggio storicamente determinato di
quella civiltà / that is, such a translator should expertly know
two civilizations and be able to introduce one to the other
through the language historically specific to that civilization."
The translator, in other words, has a role in the making of history. In Giulia's case, he believes it is part of her destiny. But
on August 3, 1931, to Tatiana, he rejects her suggestion that he
himself take on a translation project in prison, calling it a "progetto senza base / unfounded project."

TRADUZIONE ORDINARIA /
"ORDINARY" TRANSLATION

In reading the condensed biography of Gramsci's life in the
new edition to the letters, I came across the term *traduzione
ordinaria*. I gathered from context that it had to do with the

specific manner and regulations according to which Gramsci was being physically moved from one location to another—whether by boat, train, or some other vehicle, alone or with others. Naturally, this technical meaning of *traduzione* derives from the Latin *traductio*, from the verb *traducere*, meaning to lead across. This word, which refers to the movement of captive individuals, has made me think hard about the analogous movement of language (though I warn my students that the metaphor of movement can be deceptive, also limiting, as it does not fully capture the metamorphosis that translation really is). In order to understand *traduzione ordinaria,* the adjective *ordinario* must also be considered. It means more than "ordinary" in English, at least in the ordinary sense. A "professore ordinario," for example, refers to a professor of the highest rank in a university, which we might interpret to be, paradoxically, an extraordinary one. Gramsci embodied and enacted translation both ordinary and extraordinary.

TRADUCIBILITÀ / TRANSLATABILITY

Since I have embarked on a systematic reading of the letters, I have discovered a wealth of scholarship on Gramsci's theory of "translatability" and, broadly speaking, the centrality of the concept of translation in his political thinking.[3] When I looked up *traducibilità* in Battaglia, one of the citations comes from Gramsci's eleventh notebook: "È da risolvere il problema: se la traducibilità reciproca dei vari linguaggi filosofici e scientifici sia un elemento 'critico' proprio di ogni concezione del mondo o solamente proprio della filosofia della prassi / The following problem must be resolved: whether the reciprocal translatability of various philosophical and scientific languages is a

---

[3] See, for example, *Gramsci, Language, and Translation*, edited by Peter Ives and Rocco Lacorte.

'critical' element that belongs to every conception of the world or whether it belongs (in an organic way) only to the philosophy of praxis."[4] It was quite meaningful to find Gramsci, lover of foreign-language dictionaries, embedded in this celebrated Italian dictionary I particularly love.

COSMOPOLITISMO / COSMOPOLITANISM

The Greek adjective connected to the concept of cosmopolitan, κοσμοπολίτης/*kosmopolitēs*, is a compound of κόσμος/*kosmos* (world) and πολίτης/*politēs* (citizen): a hybrid word to represent a hybrid attitude toward identity and belonging. It was the Cynic philosopher Diogenes of Sinope who coined the compound word, refusing to give a specific answer to the question of where he was from. Cosmopolitanism, then, with its political origins, redefined and resisted notions of nationhood and the state. Fittingly, Gramsci has an ambivalent relationship with this two-sided term. On the one hand, we can point to cosmopolitan aspects of his personal background, his essence, his thinking across languages. On the other hand, he is deeply critical of the role and legacy of the "cosmopolitan" Italian intellectual. On November 17, 1930, he writes to Tania about the "funzione cosmopolita che hanno avuto gli intellettuali italiani fino al settecento / the cosmopolitan role of Italian intellectuals until the eighteenth century." He continues, "credo che ci sarebbe da fare un libro veramente interessante e che non ancora esiste / I think there's an interesting book to write about this, one that doesn't exist yet." In another letter to Tania, on August 3, 1931, he traces this cosmopolitanism back to the Roman Empire, juxtaposing the words *cosmopoliti/ imperiali* (cosmopolitan/imperial), noting again that, until the

---

[4] From Antonio Gramsci, *Quaderni del carcere*, 4 vols. Q11§47. For translation see Antonio Gramsci, *Further Selections from the Prison Notebooks*, trans. Derek Boothman, p. 307.

eighteenth century, "gli intellettuali italiani erano cosmopoliti, esercitarono una funzione universalistica (o per la Chiesa o per l'Impero) anazionale / Italian intellectuals were cosmopolitan, and maintained a universalistic, a-national role (either on behalf of Church or Empire)." In *Prison Notebook* 3, he writes of "a split between the people and the intellectuals, between the people and culture," and goes on to link the history of Italian to dominant, cosmopolitan intellectual classes who consolidated popular, vernacular languages. As a result, he argues, "with the exception of poets and artists in general, learned Italians wrote for Christian Europe and not for Italy; they were a compact group of cosmopolitan and not national intellectuals."[5] *Cosmopolitanism*, then: on the one hand, a reflection of Gramsci's upbringing, his interests, his involvement with the international energy of communism, one might go so far as to say his personal destiny. On the other hand, a term very much aligned with Catholic hegemony, very much at odds with the linguistic identity, specificity, and complexity of the proletariat classes. Peter Ives and Rocco Lacorte remind us of the problematic connotations of cosmopolitanism for Gramsci in regard to translation: "All too often, the concept of translation (not unlike language) is stripped of its political content and used to cast a vaguely positive glow of acceptance, accessibility, and interest in things 'other.' For Gramsci, in contrast, translation is always political and related to questions of revolution."[6]

TRASFORMAZIONE / TRANSFORMATION

In his final years Gramsci is acutely aware of both the transformation of his own health, as his body enters a state of deep decline and, conversely, the physical growth of his children:

[5] *Prison Notebook* 3, §76, p. 73.

[6] Ives and Lacorte, eds., *Gramsci, Language, and Translation*, p. 11.

Giuliano mi pare cambiato completamente cambiato /
Giuliano seems utterly changed to me.

Stai diventando una persona grande /
You are growing up.

Io sono molto cambiato / I am quite changed.

Sono diventato inetto a qualsiasi cosa, anche a vivere /
I've become inept at everything, even living.

His changing state is most powerfully articulated in a letter of
March 6, 1933, when he makes an example of people in a ship-
wreck, caught between dying and becoming cannibals:

> Ma in realtà si tratta delle stesse persone? Tra i due
> momenti, quello in cui l'alternativa si presentava come
> una pura ipotesi teorica e quella in cui l'alternativa si
> presenta in tutta la forza dell'immediata necessità, è
> avvenuto un processo di trasformazione 'molecolare'
> per quanto rapido, nel quale le persone di prima non
> sono più le persone di poi.

> But are they really the same people? Between two
> moments, the one in which the alternative presents
> itself as a purely theoretical hypothesis and one in
> which the alternative presents itself in full force of
> immediate necessity, a process of 'molecular' trans-
> formation has taken place, however swift, in which
> the former people are no longer the resulting people.

I read this as a revelatory gloss on the process of textual transformation as well.

TRASLAZIONE / TRANSLATION, TRANSFER, REMOVAL

How to define this Italian word in English? Stemming from the Latin noun *translatio*, meaning (among other things) transporting or transplanting, it resembles "translation" more than *traduzione* does. In Italian, the word *traslazione* is followed by fifteen definitions in Battaglia, and is preceded by *traslatamento, traslatare, traslatario, traslativamente, traslativo, traslatizio, traslato, traslatore, traslatorio*, and *traslazionale*. The first definition for *traslazione* refers to moving or transferring something from one place to another—in particular, a sacred object that is moved from one location to a place of veneration. More generally, it refers to a person (or people) who are moved. Not until the third definition do we arrive at "traduzione" (translation) as one of its meanings, in the sense of changing of a text from one language into another. *Traslazione* has a range of additional definitions that apply to the changing of laws, the formation of crystals, geometric transformation, the dynamics of waves), psychoanalytical "transference" between analyst and analysand, and finally, a metaphor or trope. Beyond Battaglia, I found yet other meanings in Italian under the heading of *traslazione,* all of which are germane to Gramsci: a criminal charge that is amended; an act of transplantation or grafting; transcription; metempsychosis and, finally, an ecclesiastical term that refers to the passage from life to death. It was my study of Gramsci that made me think hard about *traslazione*; I encountered it (as a past participle) in the new volume of his letters, in an entry that also contains "trasferimento" (transfer) and "trasportata" (transported). *Traslate*, the feminine plural past participle of *traslazione*, is the word Francesco Giasi, the editor of the volume, uses to describe the movement of Gramsci's ashes from the Verano cemetery, where they had been placed temporarily after his death, stating: "saranno traslate per volontà di Tania al Cimitero acattolico per i cittadini stranieri di Testaccio nel settembre 1938." These are the final words of the chronology of Gramsci's life in the new edition of the letters. They mean: "They will be removed at Tania's request to the non-Catholic cemetery for the foreign citizens of Testaccio, in September of 1938." My final point here is that, even after his death, Gramsci was moving from one place to another.

FANTASMI / GHOSTS

A recurring term, image, and point of reference in the letters.

SIGNIFICATO / SIGNIFICANCE

If translation refers to the re-creation, the renovation, or the approximation of meaning, then I will close by interpreting what it has meant to read Gramsci's letters and to think about his legacy more generally over a period of months, in a nation he never visited, in a library that houses his writings, his thinking, books not only by him but about him, and additional books I needed to make the most sense of his words. As my study of his letters intensified, it grew more and more difficult to cease my reading of them in the library (given that, each time, at a certain time, I was expected to leave). The letters have transformed me. In reading Gramsci in Italian, I ask myself what might it be like to transform him into English— not because the letters have not already been translated, but because translation would allow me to know him on an even deeper level. It was not casually on the go but rather, as part of a concerted and regular routine of confining myself with Gramsci's letters and nothing else, day after day, reading through them methodically, *in order*, that I have formed my own concrete relationship with him not only as a translator but as a parent, as a child, as a spouse, as someone—and is this not everyone?—who interrogates history and hopes our world will grow tolerable and just. His ghost was with me in the library as I read him in a state of isolation and understood, through him, not only the broadest possible significance of "translation," but just what it means to be free.

PRINCETON, 2021

(9)

Lingua / Language

For the past nine years I've been writing in Italian, a language I clearly love. This language has called, welcomed, and inspired me like no other. It's become a language I speak on a daily basis and use to express my innermost thoughts. I owe a great deal to those who have read, discussed, and encouraged my Italian writing, and to those who have served as teachers and critics and friends. That said, the ongoing phrase—"Lahiri scrive nella nostra lingua" ("Lahiri writes in our language")—means that Italian remains, by definition, the language of others as opposed to my own.

Six years ago, in Greece, a friend of mine gave me his beloved copy of Niccolò Tommaseo's *Nuovo dizionario dei sinonimi della lingua italiana* [New dictionary of synonyms of the Italian language] from his shelves. This generous friend knew that my pivotal relationship to Italian began thanks to a tiny Italian-English dictionary that I used to carry around with me, years ago, in order to communicate. I've always loved studying thesauri, maybe because they are such generative texts: they insist on the act of substitution, on words as opposed to a single word, on *lingue* (languages) as opposed to *lingua* (language).

In Tommaseo's dictionary, the entry for *lingua* (which comes just after *libro* [book] and just before *luce* [light]) is divided into eight sections, each of which contains a series of citations and meanings. In the first section, so as to distinguish *lingua* from *linguaggio* (which I'll translate as "speech"), the author says: "Language is a series of those words used by a given society of men meaning the same things, and constructed in the same way." He continues: "The concept of language, therefore, is less generic than that of a speech; however, at times it is used in the generic sense given to speech."[1]

Language, then, is something specific, tied to a society. But what society (or perhaps it's better to ask, what idiom) functions and survives thanks to any one language?

Flipping through the pages in Tommaseo, I encountered a great many words under the heading of *lingua*, including *favella* (speech), *locuzione* (locution), *parlata* (spoken language), *pronunzia* (pronunciation), *idioma* (idiom), *dialetto* (dialect), *gergo* (jargon), *vocabolario* (dictionary), *dizionario* (dictionary), *glossario* (glossary), *nome* (noun), *vocabolo* (word), *voce* (word), *significato* (significance or meaning), and *senso* (sense or meaning). Toward the end of the entry, I found the most interesting citations: *tradurre* (translate), *traslatare* (transfer or translate), *recare* (bring or carry), *volgarizzare* (popularize), *voltare* (turn), *volgere* (direct or turn into), *rendere* (render). This list, in

---

[1] "Lingua è la serie di quelle parole che sono adoperate nel medesimo senso da una società di uomini, e al medesimo modo costrutte ... Lingua, dunque, è meno generico di linguaggio; ma stavolta usasi nel senso generale che è dato a linguaggio."

particular, has a great deal to do with *lingue*—languages in general—and far less to do with *lingua*—any one language in particular. They have to do with mutation, and thus with instability: what happens when we open the floodgates between one language and another.

In the final citation regarding translation, Tommaseo concludes: "Through keen attention to what others say, and by meditating on what he says himself, as well as on virtuous acts of candor, a great writer comes to find, either instinctively or after a brief investigation, the one word that renders the shape of his thinking, the degree of his feeling. Without thinking about translation, it is said that the word and manner of one language renders those of another: it renders them to the letter, it renders them in spirit, it renders them at their deepest root."[2]

Tommaseo's subtle reflection reveals the orientation, inclination, and spirit of a translator: a person who never deals with only one *lingua*. Though he was involved in the debate over Italy's national language, he considered himself a bilingual poet, more Latin than Italian by inclination, and pushed by nature beyond any *lingua* of his own. He had perfect French and translated various Latin texts, including Virgil's *Bucolics* and *Georgics*. In addition to his strong identification with Latin, he felt "greco col cuore" (Greek with his heart);[3] he visited Corfu

---

[2] "Il grande scrittore per forza d'osservazione sul dire altrui, di meditazione sul proprio e d'atti virtuosi di sincerità, perviene a trovare, o di lancio, o dopo breve indagine, la parola che rende per l'appunto la piega del suo pensiero, il grado del suo sentimento. Senza pensare a traduzione, dicesi che la parola o il modo d'una lingua rende quelli d'un'altra, li rende alla lettera, li rende nello spirito, li rende nella radice intima." (Translations of Tommaseo in collaboration with Alessandro Giammei.)

[3] Cited in Tommaseo, *Canti Greci*. A cura di Elena Maiolini. (Fondazione Pietro Bembo / Ugo Guanda Editore, 2017), p. ix.

(in exile) in 1848 and later married a woman raised on the island. Even before that, he studied Greek in Italy, passionately, swept up by its expressive capacity. In 1843, he translated *Chants populaires de la Grèce moderne*, a collection assembled by the French philologist Claude Fauriel. I find the triangulation of *lingue* that lies behind this project quite fascinating: a modern Greek text reconsidered and rendered in an Italian that has passed previously through French. Pier Paolo Pasolini—a great captain in his own right of "team *lingue*"—considered Tommaseo's collection of popular Greek verse one of the most beautiful literary works of nineteenth-century Italy. In addition to modern Greek, this plurilingual text contains a babel incorporating Ancient Greek, Latin, French, Serbo-Croatian, and Turkish.

Translating means understanding, above all, how words slip and slide into each other, how they overlap, how they end up producing a fertile lexical promiscuity. Even the meaning of *synonym*, from the Greek σύν/*syn*- (to express, identify) and ὄνομα/*onoma* (name), suggests a type of translation, for a translation does nothing but give a different and, at the same time, fundamentally equal meaning to a pre-existing text. A translation, like a synonym, literally creates more pathways and more sense.

I was recently perplexed by the headline of a piece I'd written for an Italian newspaper, which was intended to accompany *Il quaderno di Nerina*, a book I wrote in Italian: "Montale's crazed sunflower has illuminated my 'Italian' poems."[4] I asked myself: why 'Italian' in scare quotes? Is it because I write in an Italian that's false, spurious, slanted, nonexistent? Below the headline it said: "The hybrid pages of Bassani and Palazzeschi,

---

[4] "Il girasole impazzito di Montale ha illuminato le mie poesie 'italiane'" *Tuttolibri* (Literary Supplement of *La Stampa*), June 5, 2021.

Pavese and Levi have made me love your language."[5] It would never occur to me to say these words, which insist on the barrier between me and Italian and reiterate the problematic—possessive and divisive—of *lingua*. I won't insist too much on the fact that Italian is my *lingua*, but I firmly believe it's one of my *lingue*. Let's not forget that Bassani, Palazzeschi, Pavese, and Levi were all writers astride various languages, thanks to which they each formed a singular *linguaggio*, or speech, which was unique and entirely his own.[6] And yet, according to the rules of *lingua,* perhaps their Italian, too, merits scare quotes.

The history of the Italian language, and Latin before that, has always had a plural and migratory identity. What is Latin literature without the inextricable presence and influence of Ancient Greek? And how would we even care or know about Ancient Greek texts had the Roman writers not gone to the trouble of absorbing, translating, and imitating them, thereby awakening the interest of Petrarch and other humanists who, in the Renaissance, turned their attention east, to Byzantium?

[5] "Le pagine ibride di Bassani e Palazzeschi, Pavese e Levi mi hanno fatto amare la vostra lingua." Ibid.

[6] *Lingua* and *linguaggio* are both synonyms and distinct terms in Italian. *Lingua* is used more in a linguistic sense (as in "the Italian language" / "la lingua italiana") whereas *linguaggio* refers more broadly to communication and semiotics (as in "body language" / "il linguaggio del corpo"). Though I translate *linguaggio* as speech in this essay in order to distinguish it from *lingua*/language, *linguaggio* is often translated as language or tongue in English (see for example translations by Robert and Jean Hollander, Robin Kirkpatrick, Mark Musa, and Charles S. Singleton of Dante's *Inferno*, Canto 31, in which Virgil refers to Nimrod—who is believed to have devised the Tower of Babel—and repeats the word *linguaggio* twice in the span of three lines: " 'pur un linguaggio nel mondo non s'usa. // Lasciànlo stare e non parliamo a vòto; / ché così è a lui ciascun linguaggio / come 'l suo ad altrui, ch'a nullo è noto.' " (78-81)

Lingua is born and comes to flower only thanks to the sap that *lingue* provides, just as each of us is the fruit of two people, two different sources, not to mention all the other influences that enter in and define us beyond our parents. *Lingua* in the singular deceives its plural nature. I find these words by Pliny on Italy's formation revelatory:

> I am by no means unaware that I might be justly accused
> of ingratitude and indolence, were I to describe thus
> briefly and in so cursory a manner the land which
> is at once the foster-child and the parent of all lands;
> chosen by the providence of the Gods to render even
> heaven itself more glorious, to unite the scattered
> empires of the earth, to bestow a polish upon men's
> manners, to unite the discordant and uncouth dialects
> of so many different nations by the powerful ties of
> one common language, to confer the enjoyments
> of discourse and of civilization upon mankind, to
> become, in short, the mother-country of all nations
> of the Earth.[7]

Here is the passage in the original Latin:

> nec ignoro ingrati ac segnis animi existimari posse
> merito, si obiter atque in transcursu ad hunc modum
> dicatur terra omnium terrarum alumna eadem et
> parens, numine deum electa quae caelum ipsum clarius
> faceret, sparsa congregaret imperia ritusque molliret
> et tot populorum discordes ferasque linguas sermonis
> commercio contraheret ad conloquia et humanitatem

---

[7] English translation from Perseus by John Bostock. (Pliny, *Natural History* III, p. 39).

homini daret breuiter una cunctarum gentium in toto
orbe patria fieret.[8]

Here, on the other hand, is an Italian translation:

So bene che a ragione potrei essere tacciato di animo
integrato e pigro, se trattassi superficialmente e di
passaggio, limitandomi a queste indicazioni, la terra
che di tutte le terre è a un tempo alunna e genetrice,
scelta dalla potenza degli dèi per rendere più splen-
dente il cielo stesso, per unificare imperi dispersi e
addolcirne i costumi, per radunare a colloquio, con
la diffusione del suo idioma, i linguaggi, barbari e
tra loro diversi, di tanti popoli, per dare all'uomo
umanità e, insomma, per divenire lei sola la patria
di tutte le genti del mondo intero.[9]

Pliny's quote, which refers to the feminine *terra* (meaning
land or earth), puts mother and daughter (*parens* and *alumna*
in the Latin) into play: a generational dynamic freighted with
meaning, emotion, and also, in the best of circumstances, conflict. Note that in the English translation I've cited, the Latin
patria, meaning fatherland, has been transformed into "mother-
country," while *parens* (a noun which can be either masculine or
feminine, to mean either father or mother) remains a gender-
neutral parent. In the Italian translation cited above, *parens*
becomes *genetrice*, a specifically female parent.

I first encountered this passage in Pliny not long after the
newspaper headline appeared, in the context of an exhibit called "Tota Italia: Alle origini di una nazione" [All Italy: At the

[8] *Histoire Naturelle*, III, 39.

[9] *Storia Naturale I: Cosmologia e Geografia Libri 1–6*, p. 401.

origins of a nation] at the Scuderie del Quirinale in Rome. The title of this exhibit alluded to an aphorism attributed to Augustus—"Iuravit in mea verba tota Italia "[10]—and focused on the network of culturally diverse roots underlying the process of Roman unification under Augustus between the fourth century BCE and the first century CE. Pliny's words were used as a caption to illustrate the fundamental role of pre-Roman languages serving as the substratum of classical Latin. In the museum caption, the terms *madre* and *figlia* ("mother" and "daughter") replace *parens* and *alumna,* not only emphasizing that the parent is female, but alluding to the intimacy and tensions associated, potentially, with those roles and that relationship.[11]

What strikes me is that in both the English and Italian translations, the language of motherhood dominates, but to differing degrees.[12] *Lingua* is a component of the term *lingua madre* (meaning mother tongue in Italian), and it is the consort, as it were, of *patria*. I am always in conflict with the so-called "lingua madre," a notion limiting in and of itself, and irrelevant for many. The word *patria*, in my case, is even more alienating. As soon as I shift toward *lingue* I'm less anxious; that's where I find a network of wider, friendlier relations based not only on mother and daughter but also involving aunt, grandmother, cousin, and granddaughter.[13]

[10] The full citation is "Iurauit in mea verta tota Italia sponte sua et me belli, quo vici ad Actium, ducem depoposcit" ("All of Italy willingly swore an oath to me and requested me as leader in the war at Actium in which I prevailed"). In *Res gestae divi Augusti* [The achievements of the deified Augusti], 25.

[11] Caption, "Tota Italia: Alle origini di una nazione," Scuderie del Quirinale, May 14–July 25 2021. Curated by Massimo Osanna and Stéphane Verger.

[12] I am grateful to Yelena Baraz for her gloss on this passage.

[13] I would like to underscore that these words are all in the feminine in the Italian text: *zia, nonna, cugina e nipotina.*

Pliny in his own way underscores the dynamic between *lingua* and *lingue*. *Lingua* can unite, contain, and even conquer a population, but *lingue* always has the upper hand. *Lingue* remains the backbone, the foundation, while *lingua* is labile (and according to Plato, "easier to fashion than wax").[14] I believe that *lingue*, not *lingua*, is everyone's point of origin, which is why, in the end, I'd put scare quote around *lingua*: a construction, a short circuit, a cat that bites its tail.

Tommaseo couldn't stand Giacomo Leopardi, who was his contemporary. The feeling was mutual. One can read Leopardi's *Zibaldone* as a kind of dictionary, and Tommaseo's dictionary of synonyms as a kind of relatively ordered *zibaldone*.[15] There are a large number of citations on both *lingua* and *lingue* in the *Zibaldone*; taken together, these two terms constitute one of the most analyzed subjects in Leopardi's text. I'll close with his words, which highlight the crucial connection between *lingue* and comprehension:

> Knowing several languages affords some greater facility and clarity in the way we formulate our thoughts, for it is through language that we think. Now, perhaps no language has enough words and phrases to correspond to and express all the infinite subtleties of thought. The knowledge of several languages and the ability, therefore, to express in one language what cannot be said in another, or cannot at least be expressed so succinctly or concisely, or which we cannot find as quickly in another language, makes it easier for us to articulate

[14] *Republic*, book 9, 588 d.

[15] A generic word in Italian meaning a mishmash, a compilation of confusing elements. One might argue that *zibaldone* is an apt synonym for *lingue*.

our thoughts and to understand ourselves, and to apply the word to the idea, which, without that application, would remain confused in our minds.[16]

Only *lingue* allows us to express ourselves and know ourselves. *Lingue* leads us to the infinite within us: to the spaces and the silences, to the sweet sinking into the sea beyond any nation or definition, beyond any hedgerow or border.[17]

ROME, 2021

Translated by the author

---

[16] *Zib.* 95: "Il posseder più lingue dona una certa maggior facilità e chiarezza di pensare seco stesso, perché noi pensiamo parlando. Ora nessuna lingua ha forse tante parole e modi da corrispondere ed esprimere tutti gl'infiniti particolari del pensiero. Il posseder più lingue e il potere perciò esprimere in una quello che non si può in un'altra, o almeno così acconciamente o brevemente, o che non ci viene così tosto trovato da esprimere in un'altra lingua, ci dà una maggior facilità di spiegarci seco noi e d'intenderci noi medesimi, applicando la parola all'idea, che senza questa applicazione rimarrebbe molto confusa nella nostra mente." *Zibaldone: The Notebooks of Leopardi*, edited by Michael Caesar and Franco D'Intino, translated by Kathleen Baldwin et al.

[17] This last sentence contains references to the language in Leopardi's poem "L'infinito."

(10)

Calvino Abroad

To speak of Italo Calvino's popularity outside of Italy is to speak of Calvino in translation, given that he has been read and loved abroad in other languages and not in Italian. For an author who floats, as Calvino himself said, "a bit in mid-air," translation—that twofold and intermediate space—was his destiny.

Let's start with his Italian (or non-Italian) identity, an Italianness always tilting toward the Other. These are some biographical facts (with which he loved to play): he was born in Cuba, raised in San Remo—an extremely cosmopolitan city at the time—and married an Argentine translator. He lived for many years in France and traveled the world. It comes as no surprise that New York City, a perennial crossroads of languages and cultures, was the place he considered most "his."

We should note the passion he felt, from the beginning, for non-Italian authors: the discovery of Kipling as a young man, and his baccalaureate thesis on Conrad, an author who, it so happens, wrote in a language he was not born into. Let's bear in mind his friendship and collaboration with Cesare Pavese and Elio Vittorini, two fellow writer-translators who were also editors. These are just a few highlights of his formation as a writer before achieving worldwide fame.

More international than Italian, Calvino straddled places and languages and was acutely aware of what could be mined from a detachment from one's own origins. Remember that he wrote his most mature works—those that were most celebrated, and therefore most widely translated—in France while experiencing, willfully, a fertile state of linguistic exile. He was the translator of Raymond Queneau, a French writer known for his linguistic whimsy, though I would add that *Le fiabe italiane*, the Italian folktales he collected and adapted, were also a sort of translation.

William Weaver, Calvino's American translator, says in an interview with *The Paris Review* that Calvino was easy to translate because he wrote in a literary language: a universal idiom that lends itself naturally to translation. He adds, however, that it was also a challenge to replicate the careful rhythm of his prose, and that he would read passages from *Invisible Cities* out loud while he translated. Weaver also understands Calvino's passion for scientific language and for technical terms, which pose another hurdle for any translator, introducing yet another language, one that is rigorously specific, to his writing. This is my point: Calvino, a distinctly Italian writer, has never written purely in Italian. On the contrary, he had his own language— an expressive kingdom belonging only to him—as do all other important and interesting writers.

In his essay "To Translate Is the Real Way of Reading a Text," Calvino speaks of the issue of multiplicity by referring to "different levels of language." He argues that translation "requires a sort of miracle," speaking of its "secret essence" as if it were an extract to distill with the proper equipment. He is attuned to issues of translation not only as a translator/writer, but as a man of letters who was also a scientist; this essential double nature underlies the way that he reflects on the problematic nature of translation. He writes: "True literature works along the untranslatable margins of every language."

Perhaps the most startling observation in his essay is this: that due to the discrepancy between the spoken and written language, Italian writers "always have a problem with their own language [and they live] in a state of linguistic neurosis." Calvino is able to identify this problem because he looks at Italian from both inside and outside, as if it were a foreign tongue, or in any case, like his character Mr. Palomar, from a measured distance. Calvino appreciated being translated not only to be read in more places, but also in order to "understand better what I have written and why." Translation, for him, was a form of γνῶθι σεαυτόν / *gnōthi seauton*, a revelatory process to see and know himself from a new angle, from a foreign and alienating perspective.

Invention and *innovation* are two terms often used by non-Italian critics regarding Calvino. Joseph McElroy, in his 1974 review of *Invisible Cities* in *The New York Times*, calls him "Italy's most original storyteller." In speaking of the novel, McElroy draws attention to the conversation between the emperor, Kublai Khan, and the traveler, Marco Polo. Plato's dialogues come to mind; not surprisingly, the critic discusses archetypal forms, and concludes: "If they are forms, they are also like signals condensing in themselves power that awaits its translation into form. And Calvino's book is like no other I know." *Original* is a term that inevitably refers to translation, pointing to the ongoing dynamic between the initial "primary text" and the new one, which is secondary, transformed. *Original* has to do with what is *radical* and, thus, with what is *revolutionary*. Calvino himself considered *Invisible Cities* his most popular book in America. Curiously, according to the author himself, it was also the furthest removed from the usual fare of American readers.

Anatole Broyard, who reviewed *Marcovaldo*, in 1983, also in *The New York Times,* is less enthusiastic than McElroy, though Broyard, too, describes Calvino as "the Italian writer who seems to cause the most excitement among American readers." He compares Calvino's fantastical writing to the rarefied images of de Chirico, another hybrid artist who cut across the spectrum. He also mentions critics who describe Calvino's project as an "emancipation"—a loaded term in the collective American conscience. He notes comparisons of Calvino with Gabriel García Márquez and Jorge Luis Borges, two Spanish-language writers of stratospheric impact. He concedes: "Mr. Calvino invents, but he does not persevere." According to Broyard, Calvino's most beloved book is *If on a Winter's Night a Traveler*. I see no need to belabor the apt but abused metaphor of the translator's task as traveler.

Why was Calvino so loved outside Italy? I would point to the innovative language, the imagination that roamed and pushed forward, also the use of irony. In his review, Broyard maintains that Calvino's use of irony is overvalued. I do not agree. Calvino was a master at playing with linguistic register, alternating between high and low, humor and seriousness, philosophy and fantasy, shifting from one literary genre to another. His objective-subjective gaze took in the world along with the cosmos, the everyday and the eternal.

In one of my student workshops at Princeton University, we translated his short story "Dialogue with a Tortoise," a section that was cut from the novel *Palomar*. And this is why I can confirm just how much Calvino is still loved in America, even among younger readers. My students loved tackling a marvelously challenging text containing an avalanche of scientific terms and an effervescent sense of humor. In the end, humor may be the hardest thing of all to translate well. The story unfolds emphatically in the form of a Platonic dialogue, or perhaps one by Leopardi. I believe that Calvino was always in dialogue with himself, with his shadow-twin, so as to see himself, as I have said, from a new perspective. He embodies, in this regard, the sensibility of the translator, who is always playing with two texts, two voices.

Calvino speaks directly about translation—a distinctly and exclusively human venture—in "Dialogue with a Tortoise." Palomar tells the creature: "But even if we could prove that thoughts exist inside your retractable head, I must take the liberty of translating it into words to allow it to exist for others as well, besides yourself. Just as I am doing at this moment: lending you a language so that you can think your thoughts."[1]

In the workshop, I realized that the desire to translate Calvino, and to do it well, is born from his own precise language, which is never ambiguous, which serves as a solid mooring in the always ambiguous experience of translation—an act that remains, in the best of circumstances, an exploration. As the students and I tackled the text, we asked ourselves what Calvino would have made of Google Translate and other algorithmic forms of converting and changing language.

---

[1] "Ma quand'anche si dimostri che il pensiero esiste nel chiuso della tua testa retrattile, per farlo esistere anche per gli altri, fuori di te, devo prendermi l'arbitrio di tradurlo in parole. Come sto facendo in questo momento, prestandoti un linguaggio perché tu possa pensare i tuoi pensieri."

Calvino's language—limpid-complex, intellectual-ironic, sober-playful—resonates in any language. Those who read it in translation find a blithe spirit, never provincial, always communicable, open to interpretation. It was his center of gravity—the floating gravitational center of an astronaut—that carried him past all kinds of boundaries and rendered him extremely translatable. The theme of lightness that he investigated with such subtlety toward the end of his life refers, above all, to his airy, multiple essence. Whoever reads Calvino in translation encounters a spirit inclined by definition toward foreign territories, or rather, allied to a linguistically porous environment.

Calvino is beloved outside Italy because the language he created contained all the necessary ingredients, that "secret essence" which produces, with exceptional results, the miracle of translation. Having had such a deep interest and such boundless generosity for other writers, especially those in translation, it seems right to me, even fated, that he was so warmly and sensationally received in the other languages of the world.

ROME, 2021

Translated by Alberto Vourvoulias-Bush
in collaboration with the author

Translating
Transformation

Ovid

In January 2021, I traveled from Princeton to Rhode Island to visit my mother. I had not seen her other than on Zoom since the previous August. I was concerned for her health; she complained of less and less energy and sounded out of breath on the phone. When I entered the house, she wasn't in the kitchen excitedly putting finishing touches on the food she planned to serve as soon as my family and I arrived. Instead, she was sitting quietly in her armchair and did not stand up to greet us when we stood before her. In the five days I spent with her, she barely entered the kitchen. When we sat down to play Scrabble, her hands kept shifting the tiles previously arranged on the board. Her voice, once supple and expressive, had drained to a murmur.

The following week, in Princeton, I took a walk with Yelena Baraz, my colleague in the Classics Department. I told Yelena that my mother was in considerable decline; that in certain fundamental ways, she no longer resembled the woman who had raised me. We spoke about the difficulty of watching loved ones age and alter. As we were about to part ways, Yelena changed the topic, and proposed translating Ovid's *Metamorphoses*, together. It would be a new translation published by Modern Library, the first English version of the poem translated by two women.

Yelena knew of my reverence for the text. The previous semester, we'd co-taught sections of the *Metamorphoses*, in English, in a Humanities Capstone seminar we'd conceived together called "Ancient Plots, Modern Twists." It had been a lifeline for both of us during the long Pandemic Fall of 2020. She knew that I'd looked to Ovid—to the myth of Apollo and Daphne— to describe the process of becoming a writer in Italian in *In Other Words*. Ever since I'd begun teaching at Princeton, the *Metamorphoses* had been an increasingly pertinent point of reference for my translation workshops, and my reflections based on those workshops generated the essay on Echo and Narcissus that appears earlier in this volume, as well as additional essays and lectures building on the theme of translation. For years I had been telling students that the *Metamorphoses*, governed by ambiguity, instability, and acts of becoming, was a trenchant metaphor for the process of converting literary texts from one language to another. In keeping with the plot of my creative journey, translating Ovid's masterpiece was the next logical twist.

That said, I had not read Latin with facility since my undergraduate years. It was one thing to pull out my Latin dictionary and look closely, now and then, at a few lines of the *Metamorphoses* in its original form. Translating all fifteen books—11,995 lines to be precise—would be another. Mount Everest came immediately to mind. And at the same time, a shiver of destiny. As daunting as the task felt, I knew that Yelena would be accompanying me, and on that cold January day, my heart heavy with the knowledge that my mother was transforming, I said yes.

We began by preparing a sample section for the editor, choosing the myth of Io in book 1—a double metamorphosis in which a girl is turned into a cow and back again. Yelena kindly arranged for me to use the Classics Graduate Study Room at Firestone Library. There I sat, alone, at a beautiful large wooden table, behind a partly frosted glass wall, before three Roman epitaphs from the second century BCE. In that room, removed from everyday reality, every edition of Ovid, every commentary, and every dictionary I might possibly need was at arm's reach. Something about the silence there, and the three Roman epitaphs, and the red Eames armchair where I would take breaks, grounded me. As in my study in Rome, there was a single window facing east. Only Ovid kept me company in that room, and I was able to keep most other thoughts at bay. I was scarcely aware of the hours that passed, and was always sad to pack up and go.

Though Yelena was providing literal translations of the text, I was determined to reengage directly with the Latin on my own terms. I therefore transformed from a fifty-three-year-old professor into my undergraduate self: once again I grew used to looking up countless words in the big two-volume Oxford Latin dictionary, studying their dense, ample definitions, and stopping to ponder and unpack the syntax line by line. A small notebook of words—an arbitrary handwritten dictionary of terms that required further reflection, another practice of my undergraduate years—began to fill up.

As is the case in Ovid's poem, the transformed individual is never free of the former consciousness. And so I was constantly reminded of the degree to which my Latin had faded. Like Ovid's poem, which insists on hybridity, Latin was both old and new, in turns familiar and confounding. I'd forgotten entirely about deponent verbs and future participles. But I soon realized that something had changed, and that I was reading

Latin differently compared to my college years. Now, more often than consulting an English-Latin dictionary, I turned to an Italian-Latin one. In my notebook, the definitions I jotted down were all in Italian, a language which is of course a direct metamorphosis of Latin itself. For, though the objective was to translate Ovid into English, I now had a new linguistic point of entry that positioned me closer to Latin than ever before. The itinerary of my translation was no longer point-to-point but triangulated, given that I was now reading him, instinctively, with an Italian brain. The process felt richer, more intimate, more revelatory, and even more satisfying.

Though I read slowly and haltingly, I also fell headlong into the poem, as if swept up myself in the current of the River Peneus that boldly opens the Io episode: "churning with frothy waves and tossing up clouds / as it cascades down, releasing a faint mist / that showers the treetops with spray / and assails distant regions with its thunder."[1] I remembered the excitement, decades ago, of encountering Ovid's figurative language, his textual playfulness, his descriptions of nature. I marveled at all the words that defined the sea and the sky. I was struck by descriptions of aching states of separation between parents and children.

Once a week, usually on Friday afternoons, Yelena and I would meet and discuss the lines we'd prepared, masked at opposite ends of a table in the Classics Library in East Pyne Hall. This, too, felt both old and new, and it also felt mildly transgressive; with only a handful of professors on campus, all of us rigorously abiding to testing protocols and social distancing rules, it was the only consistent in-person contact I'd had with a

---

[1] "spumosis uoluitur undis / deiectuque graui tenues agitantia fumos / nubila conducit summisque aspergine siluis / impluit et sonitu plus quam uicina fatigat" (*Met.* 1.570–73).

colleague in a year. We questioned and discussed and corrected and adjusted the translation-in-progress, flagging troubling bits to return to. We talked about how to resolve Ovid's penchant for using multiple names or epithets to identify characters, how to translate acts of sexual violence. We talked about how to reproduce the alliteration that runs rampant in the poem, how to honor golden lines. We looked at ancient atlases to trace the coordinates of Ovid's inventive geography.

By early March, we had made it to the myth of Apollo and Daphne, which resonated with me in particular. As I've said earlier, I had drawn on that myth, in which a nymph is turned into a laurel tree to maintain her freedom, to describe the process of shifting from writing in English to Italian. One day, sitting in the armchair and peering through the grille of the heating unit, a small yellow label caught my eye. Examining it closely, I realized it covered an on-off lever, and was stunned to discover that there was a word written on it: Apollo. It was the name of the company that fabricated the heater. The healing god.

I felt protected not only by the beautiful, spartan, and ghostly room, but by the beauty of the poem itself. The Latin contained me like Peneus's *penetralia*, his innermost chamber, even though, as a translator, I had to swim away from it. It occurred to me that the letters in Ovid, rearranged, spell *void*.

I started visiting the Classics Graduate Study Room nearly every day of the week, and often on weekends. The more I intuited my mother's end, the more galvanizing it felt to be at the start of a long translation, a project that would take several years and the conclusion of which was far beyond my sight. And the more I feared my mother was slipping away, the more I felt comforted by those three gray inscribed tablets looking over my shoulder, honoring four souls—two male, two female—dedicated to the spirits of the dead, *dis manibus*: Primus Apollinaris (who lived twenty-two years, eight months), Venustus (who lived eight years, four months, fifteen days), Aurelia Iusta, and Artellia Myrtale. All three tablets were dedicated by Roman family members: by a mother, a sister, a husband, an unspecified relative. It struck me that Aurelia Iusta's epitaph, at the center, was made by herself while still alive: *Se biva fecit*[2] ("while still alive … [she] made this"), to commemorate herself, her husband, and her son.

One day as I was translating in that room, my mother called me. It was a FaceTime call; for several weeks, she could only communicate if she could see my face, perhaps because she was aided by my image and expressions. As we were speaking that day, my father turned on the microwave in their kitchen, and because a space heater was also running, all the lights temporarily went out in their apartment. As my father went down to the basement, guided by a flashlight, to flip the switches on the fuse box, I looked at my mother's face on my cellphone screen, floating in a pool of darkness. It was one of many premonitions I was to feel in the final weeks of my mother's life, including a perfect hole that mysteriously formed in the middle of a bar of white hand soap in my bathroom, and a violent wind that flattened the peonies and shook the petals off the rosebushes in our garden. By then I was so ensconced inside the *Metamorphoses* that everything seemed Ovidian. The wind that coursed through Princeton evoked "horrifer [chilling] Boreas"; the unsettling dark hole in the white bar of soap summoned Callisto and Arcas snatched up "in a wind-born void," and paradoxically suggested even a microscopic version of the primordial chaos described in the Creation: "a rough, unprocessed mass, nothing but an inert clump heaped together in one spot."[3]

---

[2] Both the spelling (*biva* for *viva*) and the non-standard grammar of the inscription seem to offer clues about the dedicant's social class or ethnic background.

[3] "raptos per inania uento" (2.506); "rudis indigestaque moles /

By the middle of March, more and more people I knew were getting vaccinated against the coronavirus, and the snow that had covered Princeton for nearly a month was finally beginning to melt. The emerging crocuses did not console me, nor did that collective, growing sense of hope. Only Ovid did. Only a poem in which humans, or human-like beings, were transforming page after page into stone, stars, animals, plants, water, and other elements, made sense. Only those myths and legends that Ovid translated and transformed in his own right, from previous incarnations, contained meaning. Only that liminal zone where identity is reshaped and redefined. Translating the *Metamorphoses* was not only resurrecting my Latin, but reminding me that there is no plot without change.

In late March, I traveled to Rhode Island to visit my mother in the hospital—the same hospital in which she gave birth to my sister in 1974 and became a mother for the second time. She had been admitted a few days earlier, when her doctor, after observing her at home during a telehealth appointment, wanted to rule out the possibility of a stroke. She had not had a stroke. Instead, tests revealed that there was too much carbon dioxide in her blood, and we were told that her life was ending. I both accepted and did not accept this fact. For though I knew that her time was limited, I kept thinking to myself, she's not dying as much as becoming something else. In the face of death, the *Metamorphoses* had completely altered my perspective. Every transformation in the poem now assumed a new shade of meaning. Though certain beings do die in Ovid, the vast majority cease to be one thing but become something else. I was convinced that it was the inevitable passage from life to death that Ovid was recounting and representing again and again in order to enable us, his readers, to bear the inevitable loss of others.

nec quidquam nisi pondus iners congestaque eodem" (1.7–8).

We were told, in my mother's final days, to read a booklet that would help us to interpret the signs of her bodily transformation. We studied the color of her nails, the temperature of her skin, her insatiable thirst, her voice, which had dwindled to a whisper. Each alteration felt astonishing in its own way. I kept thinking of Ovid, and how charged each moment of transition is; charged due to its very precision. The narrative slows down and verb tense often changes from past to present as the metamorphosis, bristling with specificity, commands the reader's attention. As my mother's penmanship became inscrutable, as her already compromised speech dwindled from brief sentences to words to near silence, I thought of the many characters in the poem—more often than not women—who are deprived of language. I wanted to pray for her but knew no prayers. The first line of the *Metamorphoses,* which I'd write on the blackboard the first day of my translation workshops, which I've cited earlier in writing about Domenico Starnone, became one. I memorized it and kept saying it in my head, hoping it would accompany her: "In nova fert animus mutatas dicere formas / corpora."[4]

On the day we brought my mother home from the hospital, four days before she died, I followed her in the ambulance by car, stopping off to buy two potted plants—a hydrangea and a daffodil—to keep her company.[5] My mother loved plants, and they always thrived under her care. After arranging them on her dressing table, I asked her if she liked them. She immediately replied, pointing, that she would continue to dwell inside

---

[4] "My soul stirs to speak of forms changed into new bodies."

[5] Only now, as I write this, does it occur to me that the daffodil, belonging to the genus Narcissus, was embedded in Ovid: "croceum pro corpore florem / inueniunt foliis medium cingentibus albis" ("in the body's place was a golden-yellow flower, / and they found white petals girding its center"), (*Met.* 3.509-10).

them. She said this with a calm conviction. It was as if she had intuited the force of Ovid's poetry that was flowing like an antidote through my veins. Her words to me that day turned her, too, into a version of Daphne, reinforcing our bond, and they enable me to translate her unalterable absence into everything that is green and rooted under the sun.

ROME, 2021

(ACKNOWLEDGMENTS)

To Christie Henry and Anne Savarese at Princeton University Press for their vision, intelligence, and support as this volume took shape.

To the entire team at Princeton University Press for overseeing the manuscript through editing, proofreading, and publication.

To Silvia Benvenuto *per l'indice* and Amanda Weiss for clothing this book with a female Janus.

To a series of treasured colleagues, editors, writers, scholars, translators, and friends, at Princeton University and elsewhere, for shaping, guiding, and sustaining my journey as a translator and/or for inspiring and fine-tuning these essays: David Bellos, Sandra Bermann, Luigi Brioschi, Leonardo Colombati, Marco Delogu, Tiziana De Rogatis, Teresa Fiore, Antonella Francini, Ombretta Frau, Romolo Gandolfo, Samantha Gillison, Barbara Graziosi, Gioia Guerzoni, Larissa Kyzer, Tiziana Lo Porto, Jenny McPhee, Michael Moore, Neel Mukherjee, Paul Muldoon, Idra Novey, Fabio Pedone, Giulia Pietrosanti, Silvio Pons, Anita Raja, Frederika Randall (1948–2020), Michael Reynolds, Tiziana Rinaldi-Castro, Stella Sacchini, Sara Teardo, and Enrico Terrinoni.

To Yelena Baraz in particular: Virgil to my Dante in Ovid's wondrous woods.

To David T. Jenkins for allowing me access to the Classics Graduate Study Room at Firestone Library, *locus amoenus semper et in aeternum*.

To William R. Dingee for his meticulous work in checking the Ancient Greek and Latin citations and references, and for his illuminating gloss of Heraclitus.

To Chiara Benetollo for generously and impeccably combing through Gramsci's letters in both Italian and English.

To my anonymous readers for their early feedback.

To Nina Mesfin at *The New Yorker* for correcting Catullus et alia.

To Eric Simonoff, agent *fidelissimus* and Classics major at Princeton.

To Alessandro Giammei: *altro AG cruciale della mia vita nonché pilastro di questo libro*.

To Domenico Starnone *che mi ha trasformata in traduttrice, con ammirazione e amicizia*.

To Molly O'Brien for translating my three last metaphors.

To Alberto Vourvoulias-Bush for translating and marrying me.

To Amar K. Lahiri, legendary librarian and early aficionado of foreign dictionaries.

To my translation students at Princeton University who have taught me so much.

(NOTES ON THE ESSAYS)

"Why Italian?" was written in Italian and delivered as a speech, "Tre ultime metafore" [Three last metaphors], upon the conferral of a *Laurea honoris causa* (honorary degree) in the teaching of Italian Language and Culture at the University for Foreigners of Siena, Italy, April 21, 2015. The speech was subsequently published in Italian in *Made in Italy e cultura: Indagine sull'identità italiana contemporanea* [Made in Italy and culture: An investigation of Italian contemporary literature], edited by Daniele Balicco (Palermo: G. B. Palumbo Editore, 2016).

"Containers" was first published as the introduction to the English translation of the novel *Ties* (*Lacci*) by Domenico Starnone (New York: Europa Editions, 2017). An excerpt was published on the website Literary Hub, March 7, 2017.

"Juxtaposition" was first published as the introduction to the English translation of the novel *Trick* (*Scherzetto*) by Domenico Starnone (New York: Europa Editions, 2018).

"In Praise of Echo" was written in English and translated into Italian by Tiziana Lo Porto, in collaboration with the author, for delivery as the keynote address for the opening of the 2019–20 academic year at Luiss University, Rome, Italy. It was first delivered in English as the Valentine Giamatti Lecture at Mount Holyoke College on November 21, 2019, and then as the 2021 Sebald Lecture, British Center for Literary Translation, University of East Anglia, UK, on June 2, 2021.

"An Ode to the Mighty Optative" was written in English and delivered as part of the 14th Annual Humanities Colloquium, "Things as They Should Be? A Question for the Humanities," Princeton Humanities Council, Princeton University, September 9, 2020.

"Where I Find Myself," written in English and Italian, was first published in English in the online magazine *Words Without Borders*, April 2021. An Italian translation by Domenico Starnone, "Traduttrice di me stessa" [Translator of myself], was published in *Internazionale*, June 24, 2021, and appears in the appendix.

"Substitution" was first published as the afterword to the English translation of the novel *Trust* (*Confidenza*) by Domenico Starnone (New York: Europa Editions, 2021). A version of this afterword was also published as "The Book That Taught Me What Translation Was" in newyorker.com, November 6, 2021.

"*Traduzione (stra)ordinaria* / (Extra)ordinary Translation," written in English, grew out of remarks originally prepared in Italian for a panel to celebrate the definitive edition of *Lettere dal carcere* [Letters from prison] by Antonio Gramsci, organized by the publisher Einaudi and The Gramsci Institute Foundation in Italy on April 27, 2021. A version of the essay was delivered as the keynote address upon the conferral of a Laurea ad honorem (honorary degree) in Specialized Translation at the University of Bologna on October 19, 2021, and subsequently published in *Domani*, November 5, 2021.

"*Lingua* / Language" was written in Italian and first published in *Sette*, the literary supplement of *Corriere della sera*, October 16, 2021.

"Calvino Abroad" was written in Italian (see appendix for the original text) and first published in *La Lettura*, September 19, 2021.

(APPENDIX)

Two Essays in Italian

IL CALVINO DEL MONDO

Quando parliamo del grande successo all'estero di Italo Calvino parliamo per forza di un Calvino tradotto, letto e quindi amato in lingue straniere, non in italiano. La traduzione, uno spazio doppio e intermedio, è stata il destino di Calvino, autore che resta sempre, come lui stesso dichiarava, "un po' a mezz'aria."

Ma già la sua identità italiana era un'identità sempre inclinata verso l'Altro. Basti pensare alla sua biografia (con la quale amava comunque giocare): il fatto di essere nato a Cuba, di essere cresciuto in una San Remo all'epoca molto cosmopolita, di aver sposato una traduttrice argentina, di aver vissuto per molti anni in Francia e di aver viaggiato per il mondo. Non stupisce che New York, crocevia perenne di lingue e culture, fosse la città che lui considerava, in fin dei conti, più "sua."

Consideriamo poi la sua passione per gli autori stranieri: la scoperta determinante da ragazzo di Kipling, la tesi di laurea che scrive su Conrad, autore fra l'altro che scrive in una lingua straniera, e l'amicizia e la collaborazione con Pavese e Vittorini, due autori-traduttori-editori come lui. Questi sono alcuni punti salienti della formazione di un autore che, già prima della sua fama mondiale, era più internazionale che italiano, a cavallo fra luoghi e lingue, acutamente consapevole del distacco proficuo dalle origini. Ricordiamoci che le opere mature, quelle più celebri e più tradotte, vengono scritte in Francia, mentre lui sperimentava un esilio linguistico sicuramente fertile e voluto. Fu il traduttore di Queneau, ma aggiungerei che anche *Le fiabe italiane*, raccolte e riproposte da lui, fossero una specie di traduzione.

William Weaver, traduttore americano di tutto quello che Calvino ha scritto, dice in una intervista sulla *Paris Review* che era facile da tradurre perché era uno scrittore di un linguaggio letterario universale che si presta naturalmente alla traduzione. Aggiunge però che era anche impegnativo perché la sua prosa aveva un ritmo molto fine, cosa che lo costringeva a leggere dei passaggi delle *Città invisibili* ad alta voce mentre lo traduceva. Weaver commenta la passione di Calvino per il linguaggio scientifico, per i termini tecnici: altro scoglio per chi lo traduce, elemento che fa subentrare un'altra lingua ancora, rigorosamente specifica, nella sua scrittura. Insomma Calvino, scrittore prettamente italiano, non ha mai scritto puramente in italiano, anzi, aveva una lingua sua, un regno espressivo che apparteneva solo a lui, così come tutti gli scrittori più importanti e più interessanti.

Nel saggio "Tradurre è il vero modo di leggere un testo" Calvino parla del tema della molteplicità riferendosi ai "diversi livelli di linguaggio." Dice che la traduzione "richiede un qualche tipo di miracolo," parlando della sua "essenza segreta" come di un estratto prezioso da distillare con gli strumenti appositi. È sensibile alla traduzione non solo in quanto traduttore/

scrittore ma in quanto letterato-scienziato, ossia, riflette oggettivamente sulla problematica della traduzione. Dice: "La vera letteratura lavora proprio sul margine intraducibile di ogni lingua."

Forse l'osservazione più dirompente nel saggio è questa: per via della discrepanza fra il parlato e la lingua scritta, gli scrittori italiani "hanno sempre un problema con la propria lingua [e vivono] in uno stato di nevrosi linguistica." Calvino riesce a individuare questo problema proprio perché parla dell'italiano da dentro ma anche da fuori, come fosse una lingua altrui: o almeno riesce a valutarla, come il Signor Palomar, con una certa distanza. Calvino apprezzava essere tradotto non solo per poter essere letto in altri paesi ma per "capire bene cosa ho scritto e perché." La traduzione, per lui, era una specie di *gnōthi seauton*, un processo rivelatore per guardarsi da un'angolatura diversa, da una prospettiva straniante, aliena.

Invenzione e innovazione sono due termini spesso associati a Calvino dai suoi critici stranieri. La recensione di Joseph McElroy sul *New York Times* nel 1974 a *Città invisibili,* tradotto da Weaver, lo chiama "Italy's most original storyteller." Nel parlare del romanzo, McElroy sottolinea la conversazione fra l'imperatore Kublai Khan e il viaggiatore Marco Polo. Vengono in mente i dialoghi di Platone. Il critico parla poi delle forme archetipe e dice infine: "If they are forms, they are also like signals condensing in themselves power that awaits its translation into form. And Calvino's book is like no other I know." *Originale*: ecco un termine che riguarda inevitabilmente la traduzione e la dinamica eterna fra il testo "di partenza" e quello nuovo, secondario, trasformato. *Originale* ha a che fare con *radicale*, e quindi con *rivoluzionario*. Di fatto, *Città invisibili,* ritenuto dallo stesso Calvino il suo libro più amato in America, era, secondo lui, anche quello più lontano delle abitudini del lettore statunitense.

La recensione di Anatole Broyard a *Marcovaldo* nel 1983, sempre sul *New York Times*, è meno entusiasta rispetto a quella di McElroy, ma anche Broyard lo descrive "the Italian writer who seems to cause the most excitement among American readers." Lo paragona alla rarefazione estrema di de Chirico, altro artista ibrido e trasversale. Si riferisce ai critici che interpretano il progetto di Calvino come una forma di "emancipazione"—termine carico di significato per la coscienza collettiva statunitense—e, per di più, nota che Calvino viene paragonato a Calvino a García Márquez e Borges, due scrittori spagnoli di impatto stratosferico. Concede: "Il signor Calvino inventa, ma non persiste." Secondo Broyard, il libro più amato di Calvino è *Se una notte d'inverno un viaggiatore*. Soffermiamoci sulla figura del viaggiatore: metafora pertinente, perfino abusata, per definire il mestiere del traduttore.

Perché quindi era così amato all'estero? Insisterei sul linguaggio innovativo, sull'immaginazione che spaziava e spingeva, anche sull'ironia. Broyard sosteneva, nella sua recensione, che l'ironia di Calvino non funzionasse, che fosse sopravvalutata. Non sono d'accordo: Calvino sapeva giocare come pochi fra registri alti e bassi, fra umorismo e serietà, fra filosofia e fantasia, fra generi letterari. Il suo sguardo oggettivo-soggettivo coglieva il mondo insieme al cosmo, la quotidianità e l'eterno.

Nel mio piccolo ho fatto tradurre, a Princeton, un suo breve racconto, "Dialogo con una tartaruga," un episodio tagliato da *Palomar*, e posso confermare quanto sia tutt'ora amato all'estero e addirittura dai giovani. Gli studenti si sono divertiti proprio perché hanno dovuto affrontare un testo meravigliosamente ostico in cui si trovano una valanga di termini scientifici e moltissimo umorismo che è forse, alla fine, la cosa più difficile da tradurre bene. La forma del racconto è un dialogo che richiama Platone, ma anche Leopardi. Credo che Calvino sia sempre stato in dialogo con sé stesso, con una doppia anima per guardarsi, ripeto, da una nuova prospettiva. In questo senso incarna la sensibilità del traduttore che deve giocare con due testi, due voci.

In "Dialogo con una tartaruga" parla specificamente di traduzione, operazione cruciale, esclusivamente umana. Dice Palomar alla tartaruga: "Ma quand'anche si dimostri che il pensiero esiste nel chiuso della tua testa retrattile, per farlo esistere anche per gli altri, fuori di te, devo prendermi l'arbitrio di tradurlo in parole. Come sto facendo in questo momento, prestandoti un linguaggio perché tu possa pensare i tuoi pensieri." In classe, ho capito che la voglia di tradurre Calvino, e di tradurlo bene, nasce proprio dal suo linguaggio esatto, mai ambiguo, un aspetto che funge da ormeggio durante l'esperienza sempre ambigua della traduzione, che rimane nella migliore delle ipotesi un'esplorazione. Alle prese con la traduzione, ci siamo chiesti cosa avrebbe pensato di Google Translate e altri modi artificiali, istantanei, per cambiare e convertire le lingue.

L'idioma limpido-complesso, intellettuale-ironico, sobrio-sperimentale di Calvino vibra in ogni lingua. Chi lo legge in traduzione incontra uno spirito scanzonato, mai provinciale, sempre comunicabile, interpretabile. Il suo baricentro—quello galleggiante dell'astronauta—lo rendeva oltre i confini, perciò estremamente traducibile. Il tema della leggerezza scandagliato con grande sottigliezza verso la fine della sua vita appartiene soprattutto al suo essere arioso e multiplo. Chi lo legge in traduzione scopre uno spirito per definizione inclinato verso l'estero, alleato a un ambiente linguisticamente poroso. Viene amato perché quel linguaggio tutto suo contiene gli ingredienti necessari, un' "essenza segreta" per produrre, con risultati eccezionali, il miracolo della traduzione. Avendo avuto un interesse così profondo, una generosità sconfinata per gli altri scrittori, soprattutto quelli in traduzione, mi pare giusto che il suo destino fosse di essere accolto così calorosamente e clamorosamente dalle altre lingue del mondo.

TRADUTTRICE DI ME STESSA

Poiché ho scritto il mio romanzo *Dove mi trovo* in italiano, la prima a dubitare di potergli dare una forma inglese sono stata io. Naturalmente tradurlo è possibile; si può tradurre, più o meno bene, qualsiasi testo. Non mi sono certo sentita in apprensione quando i traduttori hanno cominciato a volgere il romanzo in altre lingue, per esempio in spagnolo, in tedesco, in olandese. Anzi, quella prospettiva mi ha gratificata. Ma quando è arrivato il momento di rifare questo libro particolare—concepito e scritto in italiano—in inglese, la lingua che conosco meglio—la lingua dalla quale mi sono con una certa enfasi allontanata proprio in quanto mi era stata data in primo luogo per nascita—mi sono sentita con due piedi in una scarpa.

Mentre scrivevo *Dove mi trovo*, il pensiero che potesse essere altro da un testo italiano mi sembrava irrilevante. Quando scrivi, devi tenere gli occhi sulla strada, guardare diritto davanti a te, e non sorvegliare la guida d'altri o anticiparla. I pericoli, per chi scrive come per chi guida, sono ovvi.

E tuttavia, anche mentre scrivevo, due domande mi hanno tallonata: 1) il testo sarebbe stato tradotto in inglese? 2) chi lo avrebbe tradotto? Le domande nascevano dal fatto che sono anche una scrittrice di lingua inglese e per molti anni ho scritto esclusivamente in quella lingua. Al punto che, se scelgo di scrivere in italiano, la versione inglese leva subito la testa come un bulbo che germoglia troppo presto, a metà inverno. Tutto ciò che scrivo in italiano nasce con una simultanea potenziale esistenza—forse la parola migliore qui è destino—in inglese. Mi viene in mente un'altra immagine, forse stridente: il terreno di sepoltura per il coniuge ancora in vita, perimetrato, in attesa.

La responsabilità del traduttore è tanto gravosa ed esposta al caso quanto quella di un chirurgo addestrato al trapianto di organi o a ricondurre al cuore la circolazione sanguigna, sicché ho esitato a lungo su chi avrebbe potuto eseguire l'intervento. Ho ripensato ad altri autori migrati in lingue diverse dalla loro. Erano stati traduttori di sé stessi? E in quale punto l'atto di tradurre si era indebolito e quello di riscrivere aveva preso il sopravvento? Temevo di tradire me stessa. Samuel Beckett, nel tradursi in inglese, aveva notevolmente modificato il suo francese. Juan Rodolfo Wilcock, un argentino che aveva scritto le sue opere principali in italiano, le aveva tradotte in spagnolo "con fedeltà." Un altro argentino, Jorge Luis Borges, che era bilingue, spagnolo e inglese, aveva tradotto numerose opere dall'inglese in spagnolo, ma aveva lasciato ad altri la traduzione dallo spagnolo in inglese. Leonora Carrington, la cui prima lingua era l'inglese, si era sottratta all'affare complicato di tradurre molte delle sue storie in francese e spagnolo, come aveva fatto lo scrittore italiano Antonio Tabucchi nel caso di *Requiem*, il grande romanzo che aveva scritto in portoghese.

Se un autore migra in un'altra lingua, il rientro nella lingua precedente potrebbe essere interpretato come un passo indietro, un'inversione di marcia, un "ritorno a casa." Questa idea è falsa e comunque non era affatto il mio obiettivo. Anche prima di decidere di tradurre io stessa *Dove mi trovo*, sapevo che "tornare a casa" non era più un'opzione. Mi ero calata troppo nelle profondità dell'italiano, e l'inglese non rappresentava più l'atto rassicurante, essenziale, di risalire a prendere aria. Il mio baricentro si era spostato; o almeno, aveva cominciato a muoversi avanti e indietro.

Ho cominciato a scrivere *Dove mi trovo* nella primavera del 2015. Vivevo in Italia da tre anni, ma ormai avevo preso la decisione tormentata di tornare negli Stati Uniti. Come per la maggior parte dei miei progetti di scrittura, non sentivo, in principio, che le parole di volta in volta scarabocchiate su un taccuino si sarebbero trasformate in libro. Quando ho lasciato Roma, nell'agosto di quell'anno, ho portato con me quel taccuino. Ma l'ho lasciato a languire nel mio studio di Brooklyn—anche se retrospettivamente l'espressione appropriata mi sembra "l'ho ibernato"—fino a quando in inverno sono tornata a Roma e mi sono trovata a riprendere il taccuino, che aveva viaggiato con me, per aggiungere nuove scene. L'anno seguente mi sono trasferita a Princeton, nel New Jersey. Ma, grosso modo ogni due mesi, volavo a Roma per brevi soggiorni o per tutta l'estate, sempre con il taccuino nel bagaglio a mano, finché nel 2017, una volta che il taccuino s'è tutto riempito, ho cominciato a digitarne il contenuto sul computer.

Grazie a un anno sabbatico, nel 2018, in occasione della pubblicazione del libro, sono tornata a Roma per un anno intero. A chi mi chiedeva della versione in inglese, ho risposto che era troppo presto per pensarci. Se ci s'impegna in una traduzione, o anche si valuta la traduzione di un altro, è necessario innanzitutto capire la specificità del libro, così come il chirurgo, idealmente, ha bisogno di studiare l'organismo del paziente prima di entrare in sala operatoria. Sapevo che avevo bisogno di far passare tempo, un bel po' di tempo. Dovevo allontanarmi dal romanzo, rispondere alle domande dei miei lettori italiani, ascoltarne le risposte. Perché, pur avendo ormai scritto il libro, mi sentivo come forse si erano sentiti i miei genitori immigrati mentre mi crescevano: ero autrice di una creatura intrinsecamente straniera, tanto riconoscibile quanto irriconoscibile, nata dalla mia carne e dal mio sangue.

Quanto all'eventuale traduzione in inglese, si sono subito formati due partiti. I membri del primo mi esortavano a fare da me. I loro avversari, con uguale veemenza, mi spingevano a tenermi alla larga. Per tornare all'analogia con il chirurgo, certe volte dicevo a chi era del primo partito: quale chirurgo, nella necessità di sottoporsi a un'operazione, si impugnerebbe il bisturi? Non preferirebbe affidarsi all'abilità di altre mani? Consigliata da Gioia Guerzoni, una traduttrice italiana mia amica e aderente al secondo partito, ho cercato Frederika Randall, che traduceva dall'italiano in inglese. Frederika era una statunitense che risiedeva a Roma da decenni, in una zona non lontana da dove vivo io: la stessa parte della città in cui, a grandi linee (anche se non lo specifico mai) è ambientato il mio libro. Quando si è detta disposta a tradurre la prima decina di pagine, in modo da avere un'idea della tonalità della traduzione, mi sono sentita sollevata. Era sicuramente la persona ideale per la traduzione del mio romanzo, non solo in quanto traduttrice di estrema abilità, ma perché conosceva molto meglio di me l'ambientazione e l'atmosfera del libro.

La mia idea era che forse, a traduzione terminata, avrei preso in esame al massimo una o due questioni e, più in generale, avrei assunto un ruolo rispettosamente collaborativo. Col tono indulgente delle nonne, caso mai, come mi ero sentita quando Mira Nair aveva trasformato uno dei miei romanzi in un film. Questa volta, forse, sarei stata una nonna appena appena più coinvolta di quanto mi ero sentita all'epoca della traduzione di Ann Goldstein di *In altre parole* (fatta in un periodo in cui diffidavo di qualsiasi mio riconnettermi all'inglese e non mi piaceva affatto il ruolo di nonna). Ma sotto sotto ero convinta che, nel momento in cui avessi visto la versione inglese, essa mi avrebbe svelato in modo netto e definitivo che il libro in quella lingua non riusciva a funzionare, e non per colpa di Frederika ma perché il testo stesso, di per sé difettoso, si sarebbe rifiutato di conformarsi, come una patata o una mela che, guaste dentro, una volta tagliate ed esaminate devono essere per forza accantonate, inutilizzabili come sono per qualsiasi piatto.

Invece, quando ho letto le pagine che aveva preparato per me, ho scoperto che il libro c'era nella sua interezza, che le frasi producevano senso e che il mio italiano aveva linfa sufficiente per sostentare un altro testo in un'altra lingua. A questo punto è accaduta una cosa sorprendente. Ho cambiato partito e ho sentito il bisogno di cimentarmi io stessa, proprio come la scorsa estate quando, guardando mia figlia che faceva le capriole sott'acqua, avevo avvertito la spinta a imparare. Sì, quell'atto scombussolante di capovolgersi, che mi aveva sempre terrorizzata, fino al giorno in cui, grazie a mia figlia, avevo finalmente capito quale manovra bisognava compiere, era esattamente ciò che dovevo fare col mio libro. Frederika, vissuta tra inglese e italiano per tanto tempo, era profondamente bipartisan. Aveva capito perché ero riluttante a tradurre il libro io stessa, e tuttavia, quando le ho detto che stavo cambiando idea, non si è sorpresa. Come mia figlia, mi ha incoraggiata. Spesso accade, quando si varca una soglia per la prima volta, di aver bisogno di un esempio, e lei, proprio come mia figlia, mi aveva dimostrato che si poteva fare.

Ero ancora a Roma—un posto che non m'ispira, se si tratta di lavorare dall'italiano all'inglese—quando ho preso la mia decisione. Se vivo e scrivo a Roma, ho un baricentro italiano. Avevo bisogno, quindi, di tornare a Princeton, dove sono assediata dall'inglese, dove Roma mi manca. Tradurre dall'italiano per me è sempre stato un modo per tenermi in contatto, quando sono lontana dall'Italia, con la lingua che amo.

Tradurre significa modificare le proprie coordinate linguistiche, aggrapparsi a ciò che scivola via, affrontare l'esilio.

Ho cominciato a tradurre nell'autunno del 2019. Non ho guardato le pagine di Frederika; anzi, me le sono nascoste. Il libro è composto da 46 capitoli relativamente brevi. Avevo l'obiettivo di affrontarne uno per seduta, e fare due o tre sedute a settimana. Mi sono accostata al testo, che mi ha accolta come certi vicini, se non con calore, con la gentilezza sufficiente. Mentre saggiavo la via per rientrare nel libro e mi spingevo avanti, lui cedeva con discrezione. Di tanto in tanto c'erano blocchi stradali e mi soffermavo a valutarli, o li sorpassavo, con determinazione, per non fermarmi a pensare troppo a ciò che stavo facendo, per arrivare alla fine.

Un blocco ovvio è stato il titolo. La traduzione letterale, "where I find myself," mi suonava pesante. Il libro non ha avuto titolo inglese fino alla fine di ottobre quando, con pochi capitoli ancora da tradurre, sono salita su un aereo per Roma. Non molto tempo dopo il decollo, mi è esploso in mente whereabouts. Una parola intrinsecamente inglese e fondamentalmente intraducibile, proprio come l'italiano "dove mi trovo." Da qualche parte nell'aria, sulle acque che separano la mia vita inglese da quella italiana, il titolo originale si è riconosciuto—oserei dire si è trovato—dentro un'altra lingua.

Una volta terminato, ho fatto circolare la prima stesura all'interno di un gruppo ristretto che non leggeva l'italiano e che però mi conosceva bene per i miei libri in inglese. Poi ho aspettato, in ansia, anche se il libro originale era già nato da più di un anno e aveva ormai una sua vita non solo in italiano ma, come ho detto, anche in altre lingue. Solo dopo che quei lettori mi hanno fatto sapere che il libro funzionava, mi sono convinta che l'operazione avventata che avevo fatto su me stessa non era stata vana.

Mentre *Dove mi trovo* si andava trasformando in *Whereabouts*, naturalmente sono dovuta tornare sull'originale. Ho cominciato a notare un po' di ripetizioni che avrei voluto evitare in inglese. Certi aggettivi sui quali avevo troppo confidato. Alcune incongruenze. Avevo calcolato male, per esempio, il numero delle persone presenti a una cena. Sono passata a inserire segnapagine adesivi, e quindi a stilare un elenco di correzioni da inviare a Guanda, il mio editore in Italia, perché le riportasse eventualmente nelle successive edizioni. In sostanza, la seconda versione del libro ne stava ora generando una terza: un testo italiano la cui revisione stava nascendo dal mio autotradurmi. Quando si traduce sé stessi, ogni difetto o debolezza dell'originale diventa immediatamente e dolorosamente evidente. Tanto per tenermi alle mie metafore mediche, direi che l'autotraduzione sembra uno di quei coloranti radioattivi che consentono ai medici di guardare attraverso la nostra pelle e individuare danni alla cartilagine, blocchi pericolosi e altre disfunzioni.

Per quanto sconfortante fosse questo progressivo disvelamento, ne ero contenta, perché mi dava la possibilità d'individuare problemi, di prenderne coscienza, di trovare nuove soluzioni. L'atto brutale dell'autotraduzione ti libera, una volta per tutte, dal falso mito del testo definitivo. È stato solo grazie all'autotraduzione che ho capito finalmente cosa intendeva Paul Valéry quando diceva che un'opera d'arte non è mai finita, ma solo abbandonata. La pubblicazione di qualsiasi libro è un arbitrio; non esiste, come accade per gli esseri viventi, un tempo ideale di gestazione e un tempo ideale per la nascita. Un libro è finito quando sembra finito, quando si sente finito, quando l'autore è stufo, quando è impaziente di pubblicarlo, quando l'editore glielo strappa. Tutti i miei libri, in retrospettiva, sembrano prematuri. L'atto di autotradursi consente all'autore di riportare un'opera già pubblicata al suo stato più vitale e dinamico, al "work in progress," e intervenire e ricalibrare dov'è necessario.

Alcuni insistono nel dire che non c'è una cosa come l'autotraduzione, e che essa o si muta necessariamente in un atto di riscrittura o diventa l'editing, leggi: miglioramento—che precede la pubblicazione. Questa possibilità tenta alcuni e respinge altri. Personalmente io non ero interessata a modificare il mio libro italiano per arrivare a una versione più agile, più elegante e matura in inglese. Il mio scopo era riprodurre con rispetto il romanzo come l'avevo originariamente concepito, ma non così ottusamente da riprodurre e perpetuare anche certe soluzioni infelici.

Mentre *Whereabouts* passava dall'editing alle bozze, e diversi redattori e revisori lo soppesavano, le, modifiche a *Dove mi trovo* continuavano ad accumularsi, tutte, ripeto, relativamente di scarso rilievo, ma per me significative comunque. I due testi hanno cominciato a procedere in tandem, ciascuno secondo il proprio statuto. Quando il tascabile di *Dove mi trovo* uscirà in italiano—al momento in cui scrivo non è ancora accaduto—lo considererò la versione definitiva, per ora almeno, visto che ormai penso a un qualsiasi "testo definitivo" come in linea di massima, per quello che mi riguarda, penso a una lingua madre: un concetto intrinsecamente discutibile ed eternamente relativo.

Per il primo giorno di lavoro sulle bozze di *Whereabouts*, durante l'autunno del coronavirus, sono andata alla Firestone Library, a Princeton, dove avevo prenotato un posto, e mi sono accomodata a un tavolo rotondo di marmo bianco. Ero con la mascherina e a parecchi metri di distanza da altre tre persone, ammesse come me in una stanza che di persone poteva agevolmente contenerne cento. Mentre mi soffermavo sul testo inglese dubitando di qualche passaggio, mi sono accorta che avevo lasciato a casa la copia malconcia di *Dove mi trovo*. Il mio versante di traduttrice, concentrato sul trasloco in inglese del libro, stava già inconsciamente distanziando l'italiano e se ne dissociava. Naturalmente, nell'ultima fase di revisione di una traduzione, pare sempre strano, e tuttavia è fondamentale, prescindere del tutto dal testo originale. Quest'ultimo d'altra parte non può restare nei dintorni, come ho fatto io quando i miei figli sono andati a scuola per la prima volta e sono rimasta in qualche angolo dell'edificio, attenta ai pianti di protesta. È necessario che si verifichi una vera separazione, per quanto falsa. Nelle fasi finali della revisione di una traduzione nostra o di altri si raggiunge un livello di concentrazione simile a quel concentrarsi esclusivo, quando si nuota in mare, sui pregi dell'acqua e sulle nostre sensazioni, invece che ammirare le creature che lo attraversano o ciò che si è posato sul fondo. Quando si è così concentrati sul linguaggio, interviene una sorta di cecità selettiva e, contemporaneamente, una visione ai raggi X.

Rileggendo le bozze di *Whereabouts*, ho cominciato a riflettere, nel mio diario, sul processo di traduzione. In effetti, il testo che ora state leggendo, e che ho scritto in inglese, deriva da appunti presi in italiano. In un certo senso, questo è il mio primo esercizio bilingue di scrittura, e il suo argomento, l'autotraduzione, mi sembra particolarmente appropriato. Ecco, in inglese in traduzione e qui in italiano, alcune delle note che ho preso:

1. La cosa profondamente destabilizzante dell'autotraduzione è che il libro minaccia di scombinarsi, di precipitare verso un possibile annientamento. Pare annichilire. O sono io che lo annichilisco? Nessun testo dovrebbe essere sottoposto a un tale minuzioso controllo; a un certo punto cede. È questo leggere e controllare, è l'indagine ostinata implicita nell'atto di scrivere e di tradurre, che inevitabilmente urta contro il testo.

2. Non è un compito per deboli di cuore. Ti costringe a dubitare della validità di ogni parola. Getta il tuo libro—già pubblicato, già tra tante altre copertine, già venduto sui banchi delle librerie—in uno stato di revisione che genera profonda incertezza. È un'operazione che sembra fin dall'inizio una condanna, un'operazione in un certo senso contro natura, come gli esperimenti di Victor Frankenstein.

3. L'autotraduzione è uno sbalorditivo andare contemporaneamente sia avanti sia indietro. C'è una tensione permanente, l'impulso ad avanzare è minato da una strana forza gravitazionale che lo trattiene. Ci si sente messi a tacere nel momento stesso in cui si parla. Mi vengono in mente due terzine vertiginose di Dante, con il loro linguaggio centrato sulla ripetizione e la loro logica contorta: "Qual è colui che suo dannaggio sogna, / che sognando desidera sognare, / sì che quel ch'è, come non fosse, agogna, // tal mi fec'io, non possendo parlare, / che disïava scusarmi, e scusava / me tuttavia, e nol mi credea fare" (*Inferno* XXX, 136–141).

4. Leggendo l'inglese, ogni frase che sembra sbagliata, finita fuori strada, mi riporta sempre a una lettura errata di me in italiano.

5. *Whereabouts* uscirà da solo, senza il testo in italiano sulla pagina a fronte, come nel caso di *In Other Words*. L'assenza dell'originale rafforza, per quel che mi riguarda, il legame tra le due versioni, quella che ho scritto e quella che ho tradotto. Le due versioni giocano a tennis. La palla, che vola da una parte all'altra della rete, rappresenta entrambi i testi.

6. L'autotraduzione comporta il prolungamento della relazione con il libro che hai scritto. Il tempo si dilata e il sole splende anche quando dovrebbe cadere il buio. Questo eccesso di luce disorienta, sembra innaturale, ma è anche vantaggioso, magico.

7. L'autotraduzione offre al libro un secondo atto, ma a mio avviso il secondo atto riguarda meno la versione tradotta e più l'originale che, smontando e rimontando, viene riadattato e riallineato.

8. Ciò che ho modificato in italiano è ciò che, con il senno di poi, mi sembrava ridondante. La sinteticità specifica dell'inglese ha costretto, a volte, anche il testo italiano a stringere la cinghia.

9. Suppongo che l'aspetto stimolante della traduzione di me stessa sia stato tenere costantemente a mente, mentre cambiavo le parole passando da una lingua all'altra, che io stessa ero cambiata in profondità, e che di un tale cambiamento avevo la capacità. Mi sono resa conto che anche il mio rapporto con la lingua inglese, grazie all'innesto dell'italiano, era irrevocabilmente modificato.

10. Nella mia testa *Whereabouts* non sarà mai un testo autonomo, né lo sarà il *Dove mi trovo* tascabile, che sarà debitore del processo prima di traduzione, poi di revisione, di *Whereabouts*. Essi condividono gli stessi organi vitali. Sono gemelli siamesi, anche se in superficie non si somigliano affatto. Si sono nutriti l'uno dell'altro. Nel corso della traduzione, quando hanno cominciato a condividere e a scambiarsi elementi, mi sono sentita quasi una spettatrice passiva.

11. Credo di aver cominciato a scrivere in italiano per sottrarmi alla necessità di un traduttore. Pur essendo grata a coloro che in passato avevano reso in italiano il mio inglese, qualcosa mi stava spingendo a parlare in quella lingua per conto mio. Ora ho assunto io il ruolo che mi ero prefissata di cancellare, ma rovesciandolo. Diventare la mia traduttrice mi ha ancora più insediata nella lingua italiana.

12. In un certo senso il libro rimane in italiano, nella mia testa, malgrado la sua metamorfosi in inglese. Le modifiche che ho fatto nel testo inglese sono sempre state al servizio dell'originale.

Nel rivedere le bozze di *Whereabouts*, ho notato che in inglese avevo saltato un'intera frase. Essa ha al centro la parola "portagioie" che, nella versione originale, la protagonista considera la parola più bella della lingua italiana. Ma la frase può esprimere tutto il suo spessore solo nell'originale. *Jewelry box* non ha la poesia di "portagioie," dato che *joy* (gioia) e *jewel* (gioiello) non coincidono come invece accade in "gioie." Ho poi tradotto la frase, ma ho dovuto modificarla. Questo con tutta probabilità è il passaggio più significativamente rifatto, tanto che ho dovuto aggiungere una nota a piè di pagina. Mi ero prefissata di evitare note, ma in quel caso specifico il mio italiano e il mio inglese non hanno trovato un terreno comune.

Il penultimo capitolo del romanzo s'intitola "Da nessuna parte." L'ho tradotto come "Nowhere," che interrompe la serie di titoli con preposizioni. Un lettore italiano lo ha sottolineato e ha suggerito di tradurre più letteralmente "In no place." Ho preso in considerazione la cosa, ma alla fine il mio orecchio inglese ha prevalso e ho optato per una forma avverbiale che, con mia soddisfazione, contiene il where del titolo.

C'è stato un caso in cui mi sono tradotta in modo grosso-lanamente errato. Era un punto cruciale e tuttavia mi sono accorta dell'errore solo alla fine. Mentre rileggevo per l'ultima volta, ad alta voce, le bozze in inglese, senza tener conto dell'italiano, mi sono resa conto che la frase era sbagliata e che avevo completamente, involontariamente, stravolto il significato delle mie stesse parole.

Ci sono volute, inoltre, diverse letture per correggere un verbo che la parte italiana del mio cervello, nell'atto di tradurre, aveva reso in modo svagato. Una persona, se fa quattro passi, in inglese *takes steps*, non certo *makes steps*. Ma dato che leggo e scrivo in entrambe le lingue, il mio cervello ha sviluppato punti ciechi. Così, solo controllando più e più volte, ho potuto salvare un mio personaggio, in *Whereabouts*, dal *making steps*. Ciò detto, è assolutamente possibile, in inglese, *to make missteps*, cioè fare passi falsi.

Alla fine, la cosa più difficile da tradurre, in *Whereabouts*, sono state le righe scritte non da me ma da due scrittori: Italo Svevo, che cito nell'epigrafe, e Corrado Alvaro, che cito nel corpo del testo. In quel caso mi sono sentita responsabile non delle mie parole, ma delle loro e quindi con esse ho lottato di più. Anche quando il libro andrà in stampa, continuerò a preoccuparmi di quelle righe. Il desiderio di tradurre—di avvicinarsi il più possibile alle parole di un altro, di varcare il confine della propria coscienza—si fa ancora più acuto quando l'altro rimane inesorabilmente, incontrovertibilmente, al di là della nostra portata.

Credo sia stato importante che, prima di confrontarmi con *Dove mi trovo*, mi *avessii fatto* un po' di esperienza traducendo altri autori dall'italiano. Provare a tradurre me stessa, quando il processo che mi avrebbe portata a scrivere in italiano era solo all'inizio—ne ho brevemente accennato in *In altre parole*—mi turbava e ciò dipendeva in gran parte dal fatto che non avevo mai tradotto dall'italiano. All'epoca tutta la mia energia tendeva ad approfondire la nuova lingua e a scansare l'inglese il più possibile. Ho dovuto affermarmi come traduttrice dei libri altrui, prima di abbandonarmi all'illusione di poter essere un'altra me stessa.

Essendo una persona a cui non piace guardare ai lavori che ha alle spalle, ma che anzi preferisce nei limiti del possibile non tornare a leggere i suoi libri, ero tutt'altro che una candidata ideale, come traduttrice di *Dove mi trovo*, soprattutto perché la traduzione è la forma di lettura e rilettura più intensa che ci sia. Se si fosse trattato di uno dei miei libri in inglese, sarebbe stata sicuramente un'esperienza letale. Ma quando lavoro con l'italiano, anche un libro che ho composto io stessa mi scivola in modo sorprendentemente facile nelle mani e dalle mani. Questo perché la lingua è in me e contemporaneamente lontana da me. L'autrice che ha scritto *Dove mi trovo* è e non è l'autrice che lo ha tradotto. Sperimentare questa coscienza divisa è, se non altro, rinvigorente.

Per anni mi sono addestrata ad accostarmi al testo, quando mi si chiedeva di leggere da un mio lavoro ad alta voce, come se l'avesse scritto un altro. Forse la spinta a separarmi in modo netto da ciò che ho fatto in precedenza, libro dopo libro, è stata la condizione necessaria per riconoscere le diverse scrittrici che mi hanno sempre abitata. Scriviamo libri in un momento determinato del tempo, in una fase specifica della nostra coscienza e del nostro sviluppo. Ecco perché leggere parole che ho scritto anni fa mi sembra alienante. Non sei più la persona la cui esistenza dipendeva dalla produzione di quelle parole. Ma l'alienazione, nel bene e nel male, marca la distanza e mette in prospettiva, due cose cruciali per l'atto di autotraduzione.

L'autotraduzione mi ha portata a una conoscenza profonda del mio libro e, quindi, a uno dei miei sé passati. Tendo, come ho detto, ad andarmene più velocemente possibile dai miei libri e invece adesso ho un certo affetto residuo per *Dove mi trovo*, proprio come per il suo corrispettivo inglese, un affetto nato dall'intimità che, in opposizione all'atto solitario della scrittura, si può raggiungere solo con l'atto collaborativo della traduzione. Sento anche, nei confronti di *Dove mi trovo*, un'accettazione che non ho mai avuto nei confronti degli altri miei libri. Essi ancora mi perseguitano, indicandomi scelte che avrei potuto fare, idee che avrei dovuto sviluppare, passaggi che andavano ulteriormente rivisti. Tradurre *Dove mi trovo*, scriverlo una seconda volta in una seconda lingua lasciando che, in gran parte intatto, rinascesse, me lo ha fatto sentire più vicino, il legame si è raddoppiato; gli altri miei libri invece sono come una serie di relazioni, appassionate e all'epoca capaci di cambiarmi la vita, ma che ora, poiché non si sono mai spinte oltre il punto di non ritorno, si sono raffreddate come braci.

La mia copia di *Dove mi trovo* è un volume tutto orecchiette, sottolineato e contrassegnato con post-it che indicano correzioni da fare e cose da chiarire. Da testo pubblicato si è trasformato in qualcosa che somiglia a una bozza rilegata. Non avrei mai pensato di fare cambiamenti, se non avessi tradotto il libro dalla lingua in cui l'ho concepito e creato. Io soltanto potevo inserirmi nei due testi e modificarli dall'interno. Ora che la versione inglese sta per essere stampata, il suo posto è stato occupato dalla copia italiana, che nel frattempo, ai miei occhi almeno, ha perso la patina di libro pubblicato e ha riassunto l'identità di opera da ultimare. Mentre scrivo, *Whereabouts* sta per essere chiuso, pronto per la pubblicazione, e invece *Dove mi trovo* ha bisogno di essere riaperto per alcuni piccoli ritocchi. Il libro originale ora mi sembra non ancora completato, anzi è finito in fila dietro al suo corrispettivo inglese. Si è trasformato in simulacro, come un'immagine allo specchio. Ed è, e insieme non è, il punto di partenza di ciò che, consapevolmente e inconsapevolmente, è poi seguito.

Traduzione di Domenico Starnone

(SELECTED BIBLIOGRAPHY)

WORKS CITED

Alighieri, Dante. *Inferno*. Translated by Charles Singleton. Princeton, NJ: Princeton University Press, 1970.

———. *The Divine Comedy*. Vol. 1, *Inferno*. Translated by Mark Musa. New York: Penguin Books, 1971.

———. *La Commedia secondo l'antica vulgata*. Vol. II: *Inferno*. Edited by Giorgio Petrocchi. Milan: Mondadori, 1975.

———. Dante. *Inferno*. Translated by Robert and Jean Hollander. Introduction and Notes by Robert Hollander. New York: Anchor Books, 2002.

———. *The Divine Comedy*. Translated by Robin Kirkpatrick. New York: Penguin Books, 2012

Aristotle. *On the Art of Poetry*. Translated by Ingram Bywater. Oxford: Clarendon Press, 1909.

———. *De Arte Poetica Liber*. Edited by Rudolf Kassel. Oxford: Oxford University Press, 1965.

———. *Poetics*. Translated by Samuel Henry Butcher. London: Macmillan, 1985.

———. *Nicomachean Ethics*. Third Edition. Translated, with Introduction, Notes, and Glossary, by Terence Irwin. Indianapolis/ Cambridge: Hackett Publishing Company, Inc., 2019.

Augustus. *Res Gestae Divi Augusti*. Edited by John Scheid. Paris: Les Belles Lettres, 2007.

Broyard, Anatole. "Marcovaldo." *The New York Times*, November 9, 1983.

Calvino, Italo. "Dialogo con una tartaruga." In *Romanzi e racconti*. Vol. 3: *Racconti sparsi e altri scritti d'invenzione*, edited by Claudio Milanini and Mario Barenghi. Milan: Mondadori, 1994.

———. "Tradurre è il vero modo di leggere un testo." In *Saggi 1945–1982*. Vol. 2, edited by Mario Barenghi. Milan: Mondadori, 1995.

———. "Dialogue with a Tortoise." Translated by Jhumpa Lahiri and Sara Teardo. In *The Penguin Book of Italian Short Stories*, edited by Jhumpa Lahiri. New York: Penguin Books, 2019.

Canetti, Elias. *Kafka's Other Trial: The Letters to Felice*. Translated by Christopher Middleton. London: Calder and Boyars, 1974.

Catullus, Gaius Valerius. "The Poems of Gaius Valerius Catullus." Translated by F. W. Cornish, with revisions by G. P. Goold. In *Catullus, Tibullus, Pervigilium Veneris*, 2nd ed., revised by G. P. Goold. Cambridge, Massachusetts: Harvard University Press, 1988.

———. *The Shorter Poems*. Edited and translated by by John Godwin. Warminster: Aris & Phillips, 1999.

Cirlot, J. E. *A Dictionary of Symbols*. Translated by Jack Sage. Foreword by Herbert Read. New York: Philosophical Library, 1962.

Ferrante, Elena. *The Lost Daughter* (*La figlia oscura*). Translated by Ann Goldstein. New York: Europa Editions, 2008.

Fofi, Goffredo. "Scherzetto di Domenico Starnone è un libro forte e dolente." *Internazionale*, January 7, 2017.

Gallant, Mavis. "Preface." In *The Collected Stories of Mavis Gallant*. New York: Random House, 1996.

Goodwin, William Watson. *Greek Grammar*. Revised by Charles Burton Gulick. New Rochelle, New York: Aristide D. Caratzas, Publisher, 1988.

Gramsci, Antonio. *Quaderni del carcere*. Edited by Valentino Gerratana. Turin: Einaudi, 1975.

———. *Letters from Prison*. Edited by Frank Rosengarten, translated by Ray Rosenthal. New York: Columbia University Press, 1994.

———. *Further Selections from the Prison Notebooks*. Translated by Derek Boothman. Minneapolis: University of Minnesota Press, 1995.

———. *Prison Notebooks*. Vol. II. Edited and translated by Joseph A. Buttigieg. New York: Columbia University Press, 1996.

———. *Lettere dal carcere*. Edited by Paolo Spriano. Introduction by Michela Murgia. Turin: Einaudi, 2014.

Hemingway, Ernest. "Cat in the Rain." In *The Complete Short Stories of Ernest Hemingway. The Finca Vigía Edition*. New York: Scribner, 1987.

Heraclitus of Ephesus. Fragments B52. In *Die Fragmente der Vorsokratiker, griechisch und deutsch*. 3 volumes. Edited by Hermann Diels and Walther Kranz. Berlin: Weidmann, 1951–52.

Horace. *The Odes of Horace*. Translated by David Ferry. New York: Farrar, Straus and Giroux, 1997.

———.*Opera*. Edited by D.R. Shackleton Bailey. Leipzig: K.G. Saur, 2001.

Ives, Peter, and Rocco Lacorte, eds. *Gramsci, Language, and Translation*. New York: Lexington Books, 2010.

James, Henry. "The Jolly Corner." In *The Complete Stories 1898–1910*. New York: Viking Press, 1996.

Kafka, Franz. *The Diaries of Franz Kafka, 1910–1923*. Edited by Max Brod. Translated by Joseph Kresh and Martin Greenberg with the cooperation of Hannah Arendt. New York: Schocken, 1976.

Lahiri, Jhumpa. "To Heaven without Dying." *Feed* (feedmag.com), July 24, 2000. https://web.archive.org/web/20010707074748 /http:/www.feedmag.com/templates/old_article.php3?a_id=1464.

———. *Unaccustomed Earth*. New York: Knopf, 2008.

———. *In altre parole*. Milan: Guanda, 2015.

———. *In Other Words*. Translated by Ann Goldstein. New York: Knopf, 2015.

———. *Dove mi trovo*. Milan: Guanda, 2018.

———. *Interpreter of Maladies* [1999]. Foreword by Domenico Starnone. Boston: Mariner Books, 2019.

———. "Il girasole impazzito di Montale ha illuminato le miei poesie 'italiane.' " *Tuttolibri*, (Literary Supplement of *La Stampa*), June 5, 2021.

———. *Il quaderno di Nerina*. Milan: Guanda, 2021.

————. *Whereabouts*. New York: Knopf, 2021.

Leopardi, Giacomo. *Zibaldone: The Notebooks of Leopardi*. Edited by Michael Caesar and Franco D'Intino. Translated by Kathleen Baldwin, Richard Dixon, David Gibbons, Ann Goldstein, Gerard Slowey, Martin Thom, and Pamela Williams. New York: Farrar, Straus and Giroux, 2013.

Lucretius, *De rerum natura* (*On the Nature of the Universe*). Translated by Ronald Melville. With an Introduction and Notes by Don and Peta Fowler. Oxford and New York: Oxford University Press, 2008.

————. *De Rerum Natura*. Edited by Marcus Deufert. Berlin: De Greuyter, 2019.

McElroy, Joseph. "Invisible Cities." *The New York Times*, November 17, 1974.

Most, Glenn W. "Violets in Crucibles: Translating, Traducing, Transmuting." *Transactions of the American Philological Association (1974–2014)* 133, no. 2 (Autumn, 2003): 381–390. Published by Johns Hopkins University Press.

Ovid. *Metamorphoses*. Edited by Richard John Tarrant. Oxford: Clarendon Press, 2004.

————. *Metamorphoses: A New Verse Translation*. Translated by David Raeburn. London: Penguin Books, 2004.

Pavese, Cesare. *Stories*. Translated by A. E. Murch. New York: The Ecco Press, 1987.

Plato. *Republic*. Translated by Georges Maximilien Antoine Grube and C. D. C. Reeve. Indianapolis, IN: Hackett, 1992.

Pliny the Elder. *Storia Naturale I: Cosmologia e Geografia Libri 1-6*. Edited and translated by Alessandro Barchiesi, Roberto Centi, Mauro Corsaro, Arnaldo Marcone, and Giuliano Ranucci. Preface by Italo Calvino, Introduction by Gian Biagio Conte. Turin: Einaudi, 1982.

————. *Histoire Naturelle Livre III*. Edited by Hubert Zehnacker. Paris: Les Belles Lettres, 2004.

Romano, Lalla. *Le metamorfosi*. Edited by Antonio Ria. Turin: Einaudi, 2005.

————. *Diario ultimo*. Edited by Antonio Ria. Turin: Einaudi, 2006.

Shakespeare, William. "Sonnet 116." In *The Norton Shakespeare*, edited by Stephen Greenblatt, Walter Cohen, Jean E. Howard, and Katharine Eisaman Maus. New York: Norton, 2008.

Starnone, Domenico. *Lacci*. Turin: Einaudi, 2014.

———. *Ties*. Translated by Jhumpa Lahiri. New York: Europa Editions, 2016.

———. *Scherzetto*. Turin: Einaudi, 2016.

———. *Trick*. Translated by Jhumpa Lahiri. New York: Europa Editions, 2018.

———. *Confidenza*. Turin: Einaudi, 2019.

———. *Trust*. Translated by Jhumpa Lahiri. New York: Europa Editions, 2021.

Tommaseo, Niccolò. *Nuovo dizionario dei sinonimi della lingua italiana*. Naples: Fratelli Melita, 1990.

Weaver, William, interviewed by Willard Spiegelman. "The Art of Translation No. 3." *The Paris Review* 161 (Spring 2002).

FURTHER READING

Allen, Esther, and Susan Bernofsky, eds. *In Translation: Translators on their Work and What It Means*. New York: Columbia University Press, 2013.

Apter, Emily. *Against World Literature: On the Politics of Untranslatability*. New York: Verso, 2013.

Bassnett, Susan. *Translation Studies*. London: Routledge, 2014.

Beckett, Samuel. *Secret Transfusions: The 1930 Literary Translations from Italian*. Edited with an essay by Marco Sonzogni. Toronto: Guernica Editions, 2010.

Bellos, David. *Is That a Fish in Your Ear?: Translation and the Meaning of Everything*. New York: Farrar, Straus and Giroux, 2012.

Bermann, Sandra, and Michael Wood, eds. *Nation, Language, and the Ethics of Translation*. Princeton, NJ: Princeton University Press, 2005.

Bhabha, Homi. *The Location of Culture*. London: Routledge, 1994.

Briggs, Kate. *This Little Art*. London: Fitzcarraldo Editions, 2017.

Butler, Judith. "Gender in Translation: Beyond Monolingualism." *philoSOPHIA* 9, no. 1 (2019): 1–25.

Carson, Anne. "Variations on the Right to Remain Silent." *A Public Space* 7 (2008). https://apublicspace.org/magazine/detail/varia tions-on-the-right-to-remain-silent.

Cassin, Barbara, ed. *Dictionary of Untranslatables: A Philosophical Lexicon.* Translated by Steven Rendall, Christian Hubert, Jeffrey Mehlman, Nathaniel Stein, and Michael Syrotinski. Translation edited by Emily Apter, Jacques Lerza, and Michael Wood. Princeton, NJ: Princeton University Press, 2004.

Chamberlain, Lori. "Gender and the Metaphorics of Translation." *Signs* 13, no. 3 (Spring 1988): 454–72.

Cioran, E. M. *Tradire la propria lingua: Intervista con Philippe D. Dra-codaïdis.* Edited by Antonio Di Gennaro, translated by Massimo Carloni. Naples: La scuola di Pitagora, 2015.

Cordingley, Anthony, ed. *Self-Translation: Brokering Originality in a Hybrid Culture.* London: Bloomsbury, 2013.

Davis, Lydia. "Some Notes on Translation and on Madame Bovary." *The Paris Review* 198 (Fall 2011).

Eco, Umberto. *Dire quasi la stessa cosa: Esperienze di traduzione.* Milan: Bompiani, 2003.

———. *Mouse or Rat?: Translation as Negotiation.* London: Phoenix, 2004.

———. *Experiences in Translation.* Translated by Alastair McEwen. Toronto: University of Toronto Press, 2008.

Fenoglio, Beppe. *Quaderno di traduzioni.* Edited by Mark Pietralunga. Turin: Einaudi, 2000.

Fortini, Franco. *Lezioni sulla traduzione.* Edited by Maria Vittoria Tirinato. Macerata: Quodlibet, 2011.

Gramsci, Antonio. *Letters from Prison.* Selected, translated from the Italian and introduced by Lynne Lawner. New York: Farrar, Straus and Giroux (The Noonday Press), 1989.

Grossman, Edith. *Why Translation Matters.* New Haven, CT: Yale University Press, 2010.

Heller Roazen, Daniel. *Echolalias: On the Forgetting of Language.* New York: Zone Books, 2008.

Homer. *Iliade. Testo greco a fronte.* Translated by Maria Grazia Ciani. Venice: Marsilio, 2016.

Kristeva, Julia. *Language: The Unknown: An Initiation into Linguistics.* Translated by Anne M. Menke. New York: Columbia University Press, 1989.

Lahiri, Jhumpa, ed. *Racconti italiani.* Milan: Guanda, 2019.

———. "Thirty-Three Thoughts on Dante." In *The Divine Comedy* by Dante Alighieri. Vol. 1: *Inferno.* Translated by Robin Kirkpatrick with an essay by Jhumpa Lahiri and essays by George Holmes. Illustrations by Neil Packer. London: The Folio Society, 2021.

Levi, Primo. "To Translate and Be Translated." Translated by Antony Shugaar. In *Other People's Trades*, in *The Complete Works of Primo Levi.* Vol. III, edited by Ann Goldstein. New York: Norton, 2015.

Librandi, Marília. *Writing by Ear: Clarice Lispector and the Aural Novel.* Toronto: University of Toronto Press, 2018.

McCrea, Barry. *Languages of the Night: Minor Languages and the Literary Imagination in Twentieth-Century Ireland and Europe.* New Haven, CT: Yale University Press, 2015.

Mizumura, Minae. *The Fall of Language in the Age of English.* Translated by Mari Yoshihara and Juliet Winters Carpenter. New York: Columbia University Press, 2008.

Nabokov, Vladimir. "The Art of Translation." *The New Republic*, August 4, 1941.

Niranjana, Tejaswini. *Siting Translation: History, Post-Structuralism and the Colonial Context.* Berkeley: University of California Press, 1992.

Pavese, Cesare. *La letteratura americana e altri saggi.* Edited by Italo Calvino. Turin: Einaudi, 1951.

Prete, Antonio. *All'ombra dell'altra lingua.* Turin: Bollati Boringhieri, 2011.

Queneau, Raymond. *Exercises in Style.* Translated by Barbara Wright, with new exercises translated by Chris Clarke and exercises in homage to Queneau by Jesse Ball, Blake Butler, Amelia Gray, Shane Jones, Jonathan Lethem, Ben Marcus, Harry Mathews, Lynne Tillman, Frederic Tuten, and Enrique Vila-Matas. New York: New Directions, 2013.

Raja, Anita. "Translation as a Practice of Acceptance" ("La traduzione come pratica dell'accoglienza"). Translated by Rebecca Falkoff and Stiliana Milkova. www.asymptotejournal.com.

Richards, Herbert. "Butcher's and Bywater's Editions of the *Poetics*." *The Classical Review* 13, no. 1 (February 1899): 47–9.

Rosselli, Amelia. *L'opera poetica*. Edited by Stefano Giovannuzzi with the collaboration for the critical apparatus of Francesco Carbognin, Chiara Carpita, Silvia De March, Gabriella Palli Baroni, Emmanuela Tandello. With an introductory essay by Emmanuela Tandello. Milan: Mondadori, 2012.

Scappettone, Jennifer. "Chloris in Plural Voices: Performing Translation of 'A Moonstriking Death.'" *Translation Review* 95 (July 2016): 25–40.

Schulte, Rainer, and John Biguenet, eds. *The Craft of Translation*. Chicago: University of Chicago Press, 1989.

———. *Theories of Translation: An Anthology of Essays from Dryden to Derrida*. Chicago: University of Chicago Press, 1992.

Spivak, Gayatri. "The Politics of Translation." In *The Translation Studies Reader*. Edited by Lawrence Venuti. London: Routledge, 2012.

Stavans, Ilan. *On Self-Translation: Meditations on Language*. Albany: State University of New York, 2018.

Steiner, George. *After Babel: Aspects of Language & Translation* [1975]. Oxford: Oxford University Press, 1998.

Terrinoni, Enrico. *Oltre abita il silenzio: Tradurre la letteratura*. Milan: Il Saggiatore, 2019.

Todorov, Tzvetan. *Theories of the Symbol*. Translated by Catherine Porter. Ithaca, NY: Cornell University Press, 1982.

Venuti, Lawrence. *The Translator's Invisibility: A History of Translation*. London: Routledge, 1995.

———, ed. *The Translation Studies Reader*. London: Routledge, 2012.

Vittorini, Elio, ed. *Americana*. Milan: Bompiani, 1941.

Weinberger, Eliot. *19 Ways of Looking at Wang Wei (with more ways)* [1987]. Afterword by Octavio Paz. New York: New Directions, 2016.

(INDEX)